THE WORK BEGINS

The Teachers Of The Higher Planes
Second Book of Wisdom

Ruth Lee, *Scribe*

Copyright © 2016 by Ruth Lee. All rights reserved. No portion of this book may be reproduced mechanically, electronically, or by any other means, including photocopying, without written permission of the publisher. It is illegal to copy this book, post it to a website, or distribute it by any other means without permission from the publisher.

This book is an updated and revised version of the 2005 edition originally published by AuthorHouse

LeeWay Publishing
Wilmington, DE
www.LeeWayPublishing.com

ISBN: 978-0-9970529-1-6
Library of Congress Control Number: 2015960633
Printed in the United States of America
First Printing 2016

Cover design by Sarah Barrie of Cyanotype.ca
Internal design by David Redondo

More Books by **Ruth Lee**

Other Books of Wisdom From The Teachers of the Higher Planes

We Are Here

The Art of Life - Living Together in Harmony

Now is The Time

The World of Tomorrow

Bliss is It!

The Word of The Maya

The Making of a Scribe - How to Achieve a Life You Can Write About

Can You Pray? We Are All Here to Seek the Way

Writing in Spirit Workbook

Writing in Spirit Notebook

Novels by Ruth Lee

Angel of The Maya

Within the Veil: An Adventure in Time

Writing in Spirit ~ Jeanne's Story

Dedicated to

Those who work with The Teachers on this plane

"Work is a good thing for one's humanity—because through work one *not only transforms nature,* adapting it to his or her own needs, but also *achieves fulfillment* as a human being and indeed, in a sense, becomes '*more a human being.*'"

—Pope John Paul II

Introduction

The re-issuance of *The Books of Wisdom* from *The Teachers of the Higher Planes* marks the reopening of LeeWay Publishing, rather than a new venture.

LeeWay Publishing was created to reproduce works channeled by the extraordinary spiritual scribe, Ruth Lee, otherwise known as *The Scribe* throughout this work. She alone supervised the publication of this work in its new format and style, refraining from making significant changes to the original manuscript.

From its inception, the mission of LeeWay Publishing has been to provide knowledge urgently needed to elevate the consciousness of humanity. As a result, *The Scribe* responded positively to the request of a group of entities from the upper realms known as *The Teachers of the Higher Planes*.

Sent by a higher authority to assist all those who are ready to align their potential and take effective action, *The Teachers* demonstrate ways to heal ourselves, our world, and planet Earth. *The Teachers* provide light in a time of spiritual darkness.

When originally called to work for The Holy Spirit, Ruth Lee had no idea what it might entail. Furthermore, she knew not why she had been selected to scribe for *The Teachers*. To learn more about *The Scribe*, visit Ruth Lee's internet home at www.LeeWayPublishing.com

The Books of Wisdom are *not* written in arcane or difficult prose. The message is clear and power-filled. Anyone needing help to ascend at the end of this life would be wise to follow *The Teachers'* simple instructions and begin working as outlined in **The Work Begins.**

THE WORK BEGINS

THE TEACHERS OF THE HIGHER PLANES
Second Book of Wisdom

Ruth Lee, *Scribe*

Chapter One

The world is not the way it was,
But will remain as is until you do something!

You are not the only beings to reside upon Earth, but you alone reside within your world. No one else could live within it, as you have designed it specifically for you. The designers of the past had a very different approach to life and often pretended God was in the Earth. They felt reverence for the water and air, and worshipped the elements.

We are not at all pleased that you do not care for what was given to you, but it is not our place to comment. You appear to us to be spoiled children, but God is the father of us all and God has no problem, so we have no problem. However, God has called us to teach you manners and an appreciation for the fullest possible life upon Earth. You will begin to learn, and we will continue to teach.

If the work of this world is difficult—and it is, you can change it simply by willing it to be different, but it is not easy to gain a consensus since you are all so independent of one another. We suggest you try to get together and act as one.

The work of your life is your work. You are responsible for the way you live, but the work of the world is also your job. You must be a part of it. If you shirk responsibility for this work, you cannot be rewarded. The reward for this work is the ability to pass to the next plane at the end of this life.

The work is not difficult, but you are

You do not heed the words of elders or those who care enough to teach you. You think you are the only one to be on Earth and not worried if others have nothing. That attitude has brought grief and sorrow to *you*—not to those caught in the webs of your greed and desperate search for gain. Those caught have no more worry, but you have to rid yourself of the blood and stain from *you*. The work of ridding such criminal behavior from your soul is difficult and not done in a single lifetime.

We are here to help all of you begin a new and greater work of art. You are the only ones who can expel the hate and anger that clouds all the Earth. You are the impetus to try out alternative ways to end the wars. You are the only people to know the difference between peace of mind and insecurity. If you do not speak up, who will?

In the work of The Holy Spirit, we cannot sit and wait. We must act, but we cannot move you, since you reside in flesh more than in spirit. If you cannot convince us that you are the only one who can challenge the evil of Earth, how will you convince the High Guide? How will you progress to the next plane if you cannot do that?

We seek answers to all of these questions in order to lead you out of the dark. The darkness of Earth is overwhelming. You do not know how much you have hurt Earth. You do not know how easily you can clear it of debris. We do! Not everyone reading this can clear up the past, but if you can, we suggest you do it soon.

In the past you were You, but had so much more spiritual quality then. In this life you are not You. We see you are confused. This is your life—not the past. You are no longer responsible for the time before this life. You are responsible for NOW. If you ignore it and act as though you were here for only you, then it will be the only time you can clean up Earth. God is not looking for more polluters. The need is for those who can work and help Earth.

If you are still mired in past evils that hold you back from advancement—and you are, we cannot help you. We are teachers and can only instruct you on ways to clear the hurdles. If you do not listen, you do not learn. If you do not learn, you will fail.

Some who read this are not here to learn, but to teach. They will read this and learn from it. We see you know, but do not understand that this is the time to learn. However, the time when you, too, must teach is rapidly approaching.

If the work of this world is still not ready to be altered by then, The World will be changed. It will not be changed to suit the ways of man, rather the way of God—and all mankind will suffer. You must not wait. You must begin now to alter the old ways of harming you and The World. Earth is unable to recover, but you can.

Not everyone who can read understands, but all who understand can read the mind of God. The mind of God is not complex—rather quite simple. Not to speak out of turn, but God does not act irrationally. The work of God is not as *you* are, but God is YOU.

If you do not act rationally, you are turned out by The World. The World does not appreciate irrational people. If you appear as such in any way, you are cast into the depths of rejection, which produces dejection within you. You then learn to accept the ways of The World.

The ways of God lift your spirits and act upon you in a different way. You feel movement. You sense the difference within your mind and body as it combines energies of the universe. This is not the same as The World's acceptance of you. It is not the same to be acceptable to God and be acceptable to man. You know what God has is best, but what man has is most easily assumed and accepted now.

We urge you to take the less difficult route, which is the road to God. The roads of man are tortuous and lead you nowhere. If you are lost, get back on track. The map is easy to read, because you are the creator of your life. You know your final destination is to leave this life and advance to the next level, so why is it so difficult to persuade yourself to get back to the source of your pain and get on to the pleasure of being human?

If you cannot understand, we can help. If you do not do the work, we cannot help. This is material work you must do. We are not doing it for you. The work of Spirit is not material work, yet it is. If you ply a trade every day, you learn the best ways to do your work; but if you practice your trade only a few days a week, you are not expert at it.

We can send you material every day, but you seldom meditate. When are we to talk? If your heart aches and seldom is free of pain, why do you call up a friend? Why not call us? Your friend cannot understand *you*; and if so, the friend cannot translate the words of God into language you understand—so call us!

Whatever you do while on Earth, you are the only one here doing it. You are the only one who works the way you do. You cannot duplicate the workings of one hand, nor can you begin a new project, because all inspiration comes from God.

The work is not to begin until you are ready. You are not ready if you do not sit and contemplate the results of your actions. You know that!

All The World is not the same as where you are, but you cannot understand why that is. Since you think you are the only one who can be *you*, why do you think anyone else exists? In The World are many who are not whole. They cannot enjoy life. They feel sad and dejected, wishing to be left alone and separate from others. You are to help them. You are to spread joy—so fear will disappear.

The lonely and sad exist in the work of God, but they are not lonely in the same way as they are on Earth. They are sad because of difficulties in their work. They cannot assimilate the work of God. You are not to that stage yet, but if you cannot assimilate this world's work, how can you do the work above *you?*

This is the time to learn how to be *you*. You are not the only one to have trouble, but only you can be *you*. If your work here is too hard, we will lighten it for you. We do not want to see you fail.

In the end, all of us are the same, but for now you are the only one who is not bound for home. You are stuck on Earth. You are not in Spirit!

You cannot leave Earth now, but you can leave at the end of this class. If you are free of Earth's work, you are free to leave—but not before your time. You may not escape before then.

If you commit suicide, it is the mortal sin of being unwilling to work, so you are returned. Do not let yourself sink into depression—and life will not be unbearable. If you are depressed—and many women are, we sense you feel deep within that you are not as necessary as men. This is not true!

Men are not the only ones meant to do the work of God. In fact, men are not as capable as women in understanding the mood of God or the work. So if you think God punished you by making you a woman, think back to the time when *you* chose to come to Earth. It was your decision to be a woman. You chose it because it was more honored. You chose it because it provided more options.

Now men are not as able to deny the importance of work as women, but they are not all in agreement about how it should be done. Some feel it is best to work alone, while others admire those who strive to reach the top of a large organization—and obviously neither is right.

The truly great work is done in pairs. To work in couples is to achieve the highest degree of cooperation. If you cannot work together, try another partner, but you must learn to work together. It is the primary reason you came to Earth!

If the work of a couple is unacceptable, The World does not recognize the relationship. If the work of that pair improves, recognition is given. The respect The World pays married people is due to this feeling of mutual respect *generated by them*. If you are not respected, it is because you do not demand respect or do not deserve it.

In the end, all who work together are received before the rest of humanity. The end of the line is not the end of the line, but the reception line is very long. You are urged to find a partner and work. If that work is good, you have no problems on Earth or in heaven.

In this time, many of the same sex are attracted to one another, which is confusing to heterosexuals. We do not care whether you are of the same sex, as long as you work in harmony. In this time, many who cannot ply their trades as they did in the past beat and abuse their partners of the opposite sex. This is unacceptable!

If the work of your hands is denied or not accepted, you must begin to work with your mind and find suitable work. You are not excused from work because something happened to derail a job. You are expected to find suitable employment, or you will be told to repeat this life. We find that path much more difficult. Don't you?

In The World are many who are not as capable as some, yet continually try to copy them. These people are workers. They will be rewarded! The only people not workers are those who sit and stare and act as though this world is not for them. They will find out too late that you are here on a mission—and that mission is your life.

Only the brave are willing to experiment! The poor of spirit, the meek, or cowards, seek only what others made or did before them. We seek out those who are willing to try and have demonstrated they are willing to experiment. If you cannot shake the fear of unemployment, you will work all your life at work not meant for *you*; but if You can strengthen *you* and you act accordingly, you will be *you* wherever you work.

We are not as interested in the work of The World as we are in *you*. We ask only that you work; and if your work does not suit you, then you are the one to change it. If the work makes you unhappy, you need to sit down and analyze it to determine why you stay with it. If you need the financial rewards it provides, find another way to support your life. If you need ego and physical rewards, find more self-fulfilling work where you can gain insights into *you*.

If your job is fine, but you hate to work, you are human. The work of The World is not grinding, but it is tedious at times. That is why it is called work. Do not play at life—work at it. If you play at work, it will never get done; and if you work at playing, you never relax. It is so simple! Work when you are at work and play when you are playing—never confuse the two!

The work of The World is not as difficult if you concentrate on it. The work of the next world is not that difficult, either, if you concentrate. Why sit and stare—not concentrating—if it is the key to success?

Whether or not you agree, the work of The World must be done, and you do not get a second chance to do it. You do the work or you do not, but it is not the way of this world to honor those who work against its respected institutions, yet many do. If they harm no one, their work is respected; however, if they harm or do evil, they are returned to Earth to reap the results of their evil. The work of evil is often seen in cities and towns, but seldom in rural areas. It is there, too.

We notice,
We see!

In order to be able to teach, we have the ability to secretly watch those who do wrong. If you wish to teach, you must observe others, too.

The work of evil is not confined to one race, caste, or personality type. It is confined to those who are dwarfed by the past and unable to continue. If you attract an element in this life that cannot understand God, you cannot be with God. You must rise above elements that deny God. You must ignore that which is evil and correct all you find.

We know you are not intentionally a martyr, yet many are. We sense you know if the work of The World is good or not, but are unsure what is acceptable above this plane. In the end of The World you know, the end is not the end—rather the beginning.

You learn things here that are of great value to you later in life. If the lessons of this life are only about living on Earth, you are not helped much. Therefore, these lessons include many objective ways of improving your life here, while gaining insights into You. You will know more as we progress.

This session is not as you would like it to be, but deep enough for you to understand we are not interested in impressing The World. We are here to teach The World how to live. This mission is to be continued until the time when this world cannot assimilate any further instruction—which will be its end.

For those determined to make all of God's messages complex and unequal, we suggest you read the next manuscript (*Ed.*

Note: Book Three, ***The Art of Life****).* It will be so difficult for the average person to assimilate that you will hope it is over by the time you turn the page to the second chapter. We are jesting, but please do not act as though this material is too elementary for you. You are not the only one who needs to advance, but you are the only one who can prevent it.

Ego is self-destructive,
Spirit is the way of God,
It is your choice!

The ways of God are not mysterious! You are not the only ones on Earth, but the only ones who cannot move about freely. You are confined to the scope of your work—*and* you are not equal. That is a fact!

You chose your roles and now act them out. If a role is too difficult, you cannot be *you*, thus we are here to help you be *you*. If you cannot accept help, you increase your workload, which is not our problem—it is yours.

All are awake at the end of life, but only a few appear to be. You are never deceased, yet not aware of it. You know. You are told. You even have the power to ask for a number of years in which to do your work on Earth. So if your life is long and does not feel good to you, act to enliven it. Give up on dying and get into life. Put on dancing shoes and sing to the sky. Act like you are alive. Do not sit. If we see you vegetating every day, it makes us feel you are tired and want to die.

We are unsure whether we should argue to let you be free of life. If you wish to die, then sit. We will know then that you are done with all you intend to do here and there is little reason for *you* to stay on Earth. If your work is done or you are done with it, you may leave. It is just a matter of requesting release. No big deal! It takes only a moment of heartfelt prayer. Once the words are said, you can prepare for the end.

To prepare for the end of this life, you need only turn on and listen to the *ending material*. It is programmed into your brain. You cannot accidentally start playing it, but you can trigger it. We are now aware you have fully forgotten that it exists, so let us explain.

To die is no big problem. The birth process is long and involved and requires the constant attention of God—plus the work of many others; however, the addition of another soul to the upper planes does not entail much work. You need only ask!

We see you do not know to ask. Why would you forget that? It is very important to know—otherwise, you will linger in agony at the end.

God is not the one to say it is over. You say it is over. If you wish to repeat this lesson on life, you may decide to call it off early in life in order to begin again; but if tired of work and unable to make much progress due to poor choices, you can be freed, too. Both result in a return to the work of this life, but much work is already done. You are not asked to end a job before it is done—ever. Now that you understand the basics of death, let us continue.

THE WORK BEGINS

The work of The World is not for you to decide whether or not it is the best you could do or whether it is as good as the work others have done. Your responsibility is to do your best. If The World is not open—and it is not open now—you cannot progress from one stage to another during the same lifetime. As a result, you call up and ask for different stages to be done at different times on Earth. You should stop this practice now. You are not going to have time to do that anymore.

The work of Earth needs to be wrapped up soon. The work of the old world is now done, but the new one is not decided yet and will not be pulled together in time to stop the end of the world you know as *this life*. The World is not as endless as you are, but The World is you. You should try to end it gracefully—not in a blaze or blast of random ideas gone mad. We sense you are unable to be the only one to change the work of The World, but if you cannot cooperate, who do you think will take charge?

We are not here to supervise,
We are here to teach!

This is the conclusion of today's lesson. The next lesson is not as long, nor as deep. We will continue to develop the theme of this book, but it is not as you believe. You will not know what it means until the end—when it will crystallize, but not before then.

We agree to own these words since *The Scribe* is reluctant to be placed in the position of defending the wisdom. It is a wise decision. You must sit and meditate on what you have read. Do not rush to read the next chapter. It will be there. You are to change as you read, but do not rush or it will crack the mold of your mind. Sit now and relax—let the stillness of the mind become *you*.

Once again, we are made aware that you do not know how to meditate, thus we apologize for neglecting to show you how to do it. This is what we recommend for beginners:

HOW TO MEDITATE

Begin by sitting still. It does not matter where you are or who is with you—be still. It helps to close your eyes, but that is not necessary. Stillness grows and grows as you sit in silence.

Feel the moisture of your eyes, nose, and mouth grow, then begin asking within for help. Ask only one question! Never confuse the issue by asking for many things. Once an idea or answer is formed, it will present itself instantaneously, but may not appear right then. The answer to your prayer may come to you later, but it will arrive in time.

This is the simplest way to meditate, but if you cannot, you can at least reprogram your idiot mind by repeating:

I am in control. I know who I am and why I am.
I am not confused, I am calm.
I am in control.

THE WORK BEGINS

Once the mind grasps such commands, it takes action. *You are in control* then—and always! Never fear you will look foolish, unless you are a fool. Only a fool can look foolish. It is not the essence of your being.

In the end all is explained, but for now we seek you out to help you regain much you have forgotten. We also help those who never knew: ***Now is the time to meditate.***

Chapter Two

The work of The World is not the work of God, however, the work of man is God's work. You will be judged by the gods of Earth if you are unsuccessful, but God judges you as You are—not as you appear to be while on Earth.

When the time comes to be judged, it will be done by those who are not of The World in which you live now. They have existed on this plane long enough to be able to judge, but not long enough to be corrupted by it. Warning: You will have no time at the end to readjust your story or rearrange your alibi.

Judges will ask questions, and you will be told to answer completely—not just a brief "Yes" or "No." This is the way of God. If the answer you give to a particular question is evasive or untruthful, the court will be much set against you—so do not lie. Your Spiritual Guides act much like an attorney, but they are not attorneys. They are honest! They would not play games with the prosecutor or let you lie your way out of work you must do in order to be *you*.

When the time comes and the judge is ready to tell you whether or not you may advance to the next level or plane, you are asked to explain why you think you should be advanced. This is the time to explain that you did all you could on Earth to advance and believe you will be able to carry on well when above and beyond this world. You will not explain. What you need to do now is prepare for that time. You need to do things that insure you will be advanced then, and know why you will be advanced.

We are prepping you now!

In the eons before this, no one prepped or prepared candidates, but due to the shortage of time and limits of space, we must get *you* to the next plane. We cannot waste time or let you risk being returned to a world that will soon end. The world that ends will contain many souls who had this opportunity to relinquish their evil ways and advance now, but instead chose not to do so. You could be one, too, but why let that happen?

This emergency situation does not spring from the mind of this scribe. She does not keep abreast of the local news or what out-of-the-way writers and channels are telling the world. She has heard only one channel—beside herself. No, this is our work. We are not the only ones who are here, but we are *The Teachers* assigned to prepare all who can now climb and pass the bar.

In the work of today are many opportunities to climb quickly. The World has produced a scenario of mixed cultures and total chaos. This is the perfect time to make a difference! It takes only *you* being your best to greatly change The World. The rest is history.

When the work of today is not the way you want it, change it. You have the power to change anything that touches your life, but you may not touch another's life. That is done only by High Guides who are not much into life on Earth, but preside over earthy disputes. They will not trouble you! They are not as active as your Guides are in this life.

We are here now to straighten out people's worries and get troubled youth under control. Young people are not *the* trouble. The trouble within your societies is that you are not into youth. You are not interested in them. As you grew, you were often interfered with, so you think you should let the young grow without intervention. However, they grow wild if not shown the way of the societies in which they live. You are then responsible for not showing them the way, thus we will help you now.

In the beginning of the world in which you now live, the work of the people was harmonious. They fought against the ravages of nature, but not against each other. Now you rage against each other. This is not wise! You all live in the same world. You are all the same and unlike any other beings in the universe, so why not act as one world?

If you cannot be the star, you often deny others access to fame and fortune. Why? Jealousy is the root of evil today.

All of you are sure you deserve whatever you have—but not others. None of you deserve what you have—and that is absolute truth! So if you think someone else does not deserve good fortune, you will surely be denied such good fortune. It operates like a mirror. You see *you* in other people, and if you describe them as being a certain way—you are that way.

The work of this world is interesting. You often sit and stare at the work of others, but refuse to do it. It is not so much the work, but the worker who is put down now. If you do not share work, you are in effect saying you are too good to do the work. We suggest you help rather than watch, since it is best for all concerned.

So many people believe they should do only what they are paid to do, but this is not the will of God. God is not at all here—but everywhere, and it is not the way of God to let some do everyone's work. If you cannot work, sit, and mend. But if you can work, do it! We seek out no one who is lazy; but if you are lazy, we can use you—as a bad example.

Lazy people are the only ones who hurt the work. Those who try but fail are not used as bad examples, because of the effort they display. But if you are laying down your work and sitting without a thing in mind, you will be disturbed mentally and emotionally before long. It is the way! Keep busy, so life is free of conflicts from within.

Within the next few weeks—from the time you read this, you will notice the work of your hands is done better. You are not as self-conscious and the work flows, but others may not notice the difference. We share this with you because we see you cannot understand, unless you do the lesson along with us. If you want to advance to the next plane, work, work, work while here! That is the key to the advancement of your soul on this plane.

Always remember you chose this life and death—not us. We are not the only ones who realize this, but we are not shy about telling you of your faults—those of the angelic realm are. They are not as we are. They are difficult to spot, but exist. You will know them.

The angelic realm is the corps of angels sent to disrupt the flow of evil now coursing over Earth. These angels are not like you, but can assume such roles. Many are on Earth, but not as people; however, some are here as people. The Scribe has met several and will meet more. They are unaware of the fact they are here to understand the workings of men and women, but once confronted with this fact, they agree.

Your own life is not *that* busy or confusing. You say it is, so people will not ask you to do things you prefer not to do, but it is not true. Most of you sit and watch television. Why would a busy person do that? It is impossible to believe a busy person has time to sit and watch the pictured story of a life that bears no resemblance to your work or that of others. You are not to watch others work! You are to join in and do it. How can you join in if you are not on the screen? That is no way to live. You must get into real life!

In the past many of you lived on farms and lived outside the city, but now you live *outside* life. You do not belong. You are not associated with any particular religious group. You do not work. You sit and watch television and contribute to the negativity of the world. It is time to contribute, but not to the negativity.

You must begin to share and show what you know to be true and help others. This is the way of The World. You will be unable to advance if you do not know the way of The World. Your life is to be an example—not of who you are, but the way you should be. If you can project that image, all will say you are a good person. If you cannot project the image of greatness now, you can learn and then project it.

It is never too late to turn over a new coat of paint and determine what lies beneath it. You are not a surface or a flat plate with no depth. You are deeper than you think. You own nothing that can help you in the end of this life cross over to the other side, but you are all you are and you can help *you*. We sense you are confused, so we will help you now.

If the past work of The World is not the same as it is now, we will work on the way it needs to be. If the way is not followed, you are the one who is lost—not us. We are here to help, but not do your work. You have to do your work. You cannot hide and get another to do it for you.

If the world has placed you high, you may have difficulty thinking. You may not be able to show how much you do not know, but you can work. You are no different than the employee who slaves away all day to produce paper. You have nothing, either. You are only *you*. No one else cares if you cannot spring over the last hurdle, but we do. We want the last leg of life to be your best. We want a grand finale. No more sitting in a hospital waiting for the nurse to give you a painkiller to ease you through to the end.

Suicide is never *the way*, we want a lot of time spent in contemplation. In the work of The World you often contemplate suicide. It is often attempted, but seldom permitted, because you will harm your soul. We are not the only ones who preach this, but many today are beginning to sound like preachers—but are not. You must let the rest of The World see you are not the only one to abhor capital offenses. You must unite and fight to punish those who steal, corrupt minors or those of lesser mental ability, carry out the evil acts of others, or kill people. The world is not taking care of this now—and it shows.

You often talk about the legalization of drugs known to harm all. If one person decides to risk life, you say it is that person's right—but is it? Each life is one of many that intertwines and connects to yours. If you let one die, you harm *you*, because that life is precious and should be told "No" whenever it wants to commit suicide. You need that life and that life needs to know it. If you continue to let others fear life so much that they feel a need to escape through a dream-like haze, you have failed and will be held responsible for them.

No one is of the same mind, but all have one. You sit and discuss the body, mind, and spirit and act as though it is one, but it is not. You are the only one—spiritually. Your body is similar to that of many others and could possibly be duplicated. Your mind is similar to others and can be taught to think, but others cannot know what you think, so you do not know how similar you all are in mind.

We know how much you think alike. You all are very much concerned about the same issues. We will drop that for now to concentrate on the area in which you are all different.

Your spirit is not you, but it is. You are the only one to know about the ways of God. You are the only one who is part of God. All of you are alike, but only you are *you*. If the work of this world confuses you, you are not alone; but if the work of God confuses you, you are alone.

Sit and contemplate the irony of being human

You are unable to transform yourself. You may not end your life without doing serious harm to You, and you cannot move rapidly. How could you escape the roar of a blazing fire once it grew out of bounds? We would help you! We would increase the flow of your internal glands and help you resist gravity. You would later say God saved you, but it was not God, it was YOU!

You need to understand you are not the same as God, but God is YOU. At the end of the work *you* do on Earth it is said: "You are not the only one," but you are. You exist, create, and work in this world. You are the only one who cares about the end of this world, too. We do not. We care about Earth because God created it. You care not for Earth, because you did not create it. If you fear this life ending, you fear YOU.

If this is too complex—and the end of The World is—it is time for you to simplify it. We can help you change the parameters, but you have to put them in place. We are not of flesh. We do not have the power to institute change in your world. You, alone, can change The World.

THE WORK BEGINS

In the world of your making are many mansions, but only one of them is the seat of power. The other large houses imitate that power, just as you imitate power. You live to be powerful. You wish to be rich, so you can be powerful. You wish to be beautiful for the same reason. All of these desires are silly. You will never have the opportunity to exert power.

You are here to work on *you*—and power gets in the way. Within power is responsibility that few (if any) want. It is not fun to be in charge, but it is fun to follow. You often give up wanting to lead once you have had some power. You know it and we know it, but most people do not.

You owe people the respect they give you. You must not let power become an opiate. You will be charged with many crimes if you do.

All is the work of the mind, but the mind cannot create. You in body create what the mind devises and carries into the upper spheres. You are the only one to change the plan. If you decide it is stupid, it is. You are the only one to judge if your plan is not good. All others will assume it is the way it is because you choose it to be so.

Watch artists, writers, and musicians as they place their work before you. Do they act like it is frivolous? No, they are entirely absorbed in it. You are to act like that, because you are to be totally absorbed in *you*, too.

The work of a single player is not much, but the work of many people cannot be ignored. If your work is not good, the group will use it for ballast, but it will be used. We commend those of you who can share. The work of this world is not the only thing you must work at now, nor tolerating all others who are here the only thing you have to accomplish. You must incorporate both as a way of life. If you work and live together, you have the best chance to always be *you*, but we are not suggesting you live in communes. This has been attempted and does not work.

You obviously have too many choices. You need to sort through them and select what is best for you and your families. If you can, live as one family. The division of generations is a work of God, and if you can live as one, you are ready for the next plane. If you cannot, you know where you have to work harder.

Chapter Three

Your life is not to be spoiled
by any other life

You are not the product of your environment. You are the product of inherited traits and circumstances you have preordained. This is known as predestination, but churches preaching this are not at all spiritual—not even close.

You must be involved in the process. You cannot just show up for a church service. You are not the only soul, and you do have to help others. Since you are not the only one present, you are more likely to do your part. This is what makes a church—not the denomination, which is of small consequence.

The most important trait you possess is the trait we call 'the ability to be *you*.' If you are dwarfed or unable to distinguish yourself, you feel as though you are worthless. You must not let jealousy enter your mind. The fear of being less than others is the worst fear. You will hold yourself back and have to be returned again and again. This trait is rampant in the world now. Many have returned to act upon it, but few are. You must act now!

If the fear of being *you* is not as great as your fear of being less than others, you will not be *you*. You must balance the two and get from it what you need. We are not here now to talk about the balancing act. That is your work. You do that, and we do this. We all have our work. What you do to achieve balance is not the most important consideration, but if you harm someone else as a result of your jealousy, it is.

Hoping and praying for someone else to solve *your* life's problems will also result in you being returned to Earth. We anxiously wait for the time when you will notice others are no better at life than you are. The World is not a perfect place. It is not meant to be. It is the classroom of the ages and not the perfect environment for the virtuous. That is why you are here.

You are tested and tried. If you cannot rise above the pettiness of Earth, how can you ascend? You just do. You rise above the pettiness, anger, and jealousy. It makes you resilient. You learn that others are good at what they do, but you are also good at what you do—if you work at it.

NOW is the only time when you work. Do not sit and stare at work, but work on it and do it! Your own life is not the only life, but the majority of it will be work of your soul on Earth trying to be the soul on the next plane.

You must not interfere with anyone's soul development. If you do, you will suffer. Soul work is the only work God is into here. God will hurt you if you interfere!

We are *The Teachers*, but you are not our students. We are here to help you, but we do not do your work. We could, but we are told not to, because we would interfere with your growth.

THE WORK BEGINS

We would not intentionally do anything to interfere with your soul work. We do not want to be stunted or cut out of future work. We must do our job, and then let you do your work.

If you never do a thing, you are wasting this life. The waste of this life is said to be *"not using your abilities or talent,"* but it is the loss of the entire life most mourned. We mourn if you do not use your innate abilities to grow, because your life is then lost.

If you wish to work now, and we see that you do, you could start over at the beginning—But why? We suggest you ask for help from a spiritual advisor or friend of The Holy Spirit (such as a priest, minister, good person, great soul, or a mother) what you are doing wrong. If the response you receive is evasive, search for another who is interested in helping you regain your loss. Once you are on the right track, it is seldom long before you feel fine. We are not worried about the track, but that you get on it before it is too late to get to your destination.

If you wait until the end of your life to fulfill the wishes of your soul, you run the risk of not having enough life left in your body to get it all done. So if you have time to work now, begin today. Get out the Bible, Koran, or whatever book of religion is closest to your beliefs and read. If you read and read again, you will learn; but if you merely listen, you will not.

The work of God is displayed and not to be ignored by you. If you do, you will be here long after all the rest of your people are gone. You need to do whatever it takes to maintain a continuity of your tribe, because you are part of a tribe. Does that surprise you? We are surprised!

All people belong here. All people are part of a greater entity that shares its learning and resources, but you are not the center of it all. You are part of the outer sections. You are here to develop so you can join the inner workings of your tribe. If you do this, you are accepted. If you ignore their work or your own, you never rejoin them, nor are you missed. We anxiously await your recognition of this fact. If you cannot understand it, let us tell you of the past.

Far from the space you are in, there was a time when you were not recognizable. You were energy, but not a being. You were created to be the one to enter the third world of God. You were not to be helped—instead rather steered, so you could become…

Once developed, you would be unable to remember the pain suffered at the beginning. Now is not the time to develop all the material about the beginning—but it exists. If you do not know there was a beginning, you will not know if you belong.

In the beginning all was pure. Energy was negative and positive, but not completely balanced. You were! You caused the energy to become attuned to the forces of the work of God. You called for the answer. You asked for instructions. You wanted it.

God then asked you for the right to begin a work of art. You granted God the right to steer you into the path of a higher being. You were not asked, rather told you would belong to the tribe of _____. We will not approve the naming of your tribe now. You must discover that another time.

THE WORK BEGINS

When the work of God was sorted through, you sat on the edge and added your energy to the common group. It was a decision reached within that source that determined if you were to be included or rejected. You would have to become like that group, but if you chose, you could spin off and attempt to reconcile with another tribe. It was unacceptable to keep spinning off and trying tribe-after-tribe.

Once the tribe is acceptable to you, and it accepts you, the work of soul begins. You are asked to be *you* and not accept the teachings of others. Thus begins the age of intuitive growth. You do not ask—you are told. You are not talked to aloud, but asked many questions intuitively. It is this past that recommends you to this work now.

You sense the work we do is not the only work, but it is *your* work. That is because you have been primed to do it. You were told to work and wait, but you were not told when it would arrive. So now you are ready for work, and we are here. It is so simple once you know your background and understand the way of God.

If your tribe was here—but it is not—you could join them and pulsate. You cannot gather energy from the tribe now. You must use what you have. You have enough to get into the action, but only enough to live one life.

If you ask to return, you must split off even more energy to continue. The next life is less vital, because less energy is available, so you must conserve. You must act less rashly. The life force is less and less as you age. You have less energy, but you are more than capable of thinking about how life should be.

We are not old in Spirit, but you are. You have to be. If you came to Earth as a youngster, you would never be able to recognize the wisdom of being here. You would last only a few months. The young often attempt to burn out and shorten their lives, because it is not fun to be here—but it is. You must wait until you can be an adult though!

You must not imitate the stage when you are young. The past is not harmful—rather the memory. If your memories of youth are crowded by images of hate and despair, your life on Earth is not as you would want to remember it—and that is sad.

If adults on Earth remain here life-after-life, their children are harmed. The children of your soul are connected to You by the energy YOU gave them, but they are their own souls. You are held responsible, but *you* are not required to support them all their lives. If the life of a child is threatened, you are asked to make sacrifices, but not to give up the life of your soul.

You will never be asked to give up your life for another. If you do, you are awarded another life of ease and delight. It is not to be dull. It is a life of contagious delight and glee. So if you see someone who has no problems—and they do exist, you will recognize such a person did a great thing in another life. Only great deeds are recognized this way. All other deeds are recorded and placed on your Arcadian records.

THE WORK BEGINS

We see *The Scribe* does not know of the Arcadian records, so we suspect you do not know either. The Arcadian Records are not the only records, but the only ones relative to what you do on Earth. They represent the quiet, good times that develop your being into what you will become. They are not the large volumes that attach themselves to your entire being, rather a report on your lives while on Earth.

You must not try to read such entries as you read other records. It is a waste of precious energy and time on Earth. We suspect that those who would spend time reading about the past are unhappy with their present, and the only way to improve the present is to live NOW.

Whatever you do, do it with all the energy you can muster. Energy will wane and ebb, but never disappear. It is not enough to sit and think about work, you have to do it while you are on Earth. That is a big lesson for many of you, but a necessary one.

Women of Earth are prone to develop their psychic abilities, but not use them. Men are unlikely to develop their psychic abilities, but if they do, they use them. So which sex is wiser now?

Now is the time. You live NOW! We preach that over and over again, because you are unable to be *you*—and you wait—which is a big mistake. Begin as early in life as possible to experiment with the many facets that combine to make you—*you*, and when older, you can assume any role that lets *you* be You.

All your time on Earth is less than a moment in the entire universal being, but it is one life to You. You must not waste it on silly, trifling, imaginary ills and pains. You must try to feel vigorous all your life. It starts in the brain and descends the spine. So if your life is full of aches and pains, look to the spine. If the spine is not aligned, you must not joke about it. You must seek help. However, if the spine is not out of alignment, it is foolish to seek help since it may cause you to enter a suggestive mode of behavior and believe you require such manipulations when they are not needed and would result in damage to the spinal column.

Chiropractors cannot do much for the rest of the body, but to say they are frauds and unable to help at all is a disagreeable attempt to end reliance upon them by those who fear diminishing funds. We suggest you enter into such manipulations with utmost care, but if pain is great and you are not adventurous, you will suffer needlessly.

The world has many healers, but few are in the medical profession. The area of pain is not the same as this area of work. You must be able to experience pain if you are to be a healer. *The Scribe*, for example, can feel the sorrow and pain of others, but not actually experience it herself. This is the gift of healing. You may have it, too.

The gift of healing is considered by psychics to be the greatest gift, but it is not. The greatest psychic gift is the gift of discernment. Discernment is not the ability to see at a great distance or uncover what is hidden. It is the ability to understand. You must be able to understand before you can know. If you cannot spare another pain, you do not understand pain. If you cannot speak well of another, you do not know the pain of being talked about behind your back. These things occur, but do you learn from them?

Whatever work you do, you must do it with the enthusiasm of the novice. You must never act bored if you are not—that is the worst of wrong ways to explore the will of God. You try to act as if it is easy, but instead demonstrate it is not a good path. If it were easy, you would be enthusiastic.

Now, the time has arrived when this lesson must close, yet we have not covered the most important part. We want you to begin to seek out knowledge that is within You. You are the only one who knows why *you* are here on Earth. No one else can know, because they are here to do their work. If you do not enter into the work of The Holy Spirit, you are the only one who cannot plow through the work of the world—others will, but not you.

The holy work of God is in the spiritual realm. You are not the only beings to be under the care of God's holy angels, nor are you the only human who cannot begin another life if this one is not lived well, but you are the only person within that life who cares if you do.

The Holy Spirit is that which is within YOU. You must contact the spiritual font that flows through You to YOU. You are not *you* if you cannot connect to it. The work of this life is lifeless if you are not *you*.

We will tell you how to be you now

The Holy Spirit is not the only way of God, but it is on Earth. You are physical beings while here and unable to understand the rewards of the soul. You are difficult, unruly, and upsetting to many of the higher realms, *but not us*. We are teachers and understand the nature of the being you are, but we will not tolerate bad behavior.

You are the only one who cares if *you* are here, so make the most of it. Join your tribe and head for the next plane with them. If you wait, you will be unable to join your tribe for many eons, and the time is now ripe for you to advance with them.

Tribal Laws are unlike earthly tribal laws. We are not saying you are an Indian or aboriginal being. That is the tone of today's speech, but we are not referring to tribes in that context. We are referring to the tribes of man.

There are no more than twelve tribes, but they are not all on Earth now. The last of the tribes is here, but not for much longer. You will be unable to catch up if you idle. The tribe that will be held responsible for not giving you enough education to enter the world and leave it quickly is here now; but in the future, any of the other tribes may pick you up in order to help you ascend.

Animals exist in another realm from where you live now. You are not an animal and never have been. You will enter the realm of God as you are, but not as a human. You are the essence of this life, but not the essence of a human. You exist as you are, but You are not here. You are always in the body, but You are not of the body.

At the end of this life, you will grow into the ether and disappear, but not end your life! What you do at the end of life is not interesting—*you* are—but not the process. Why are so many people taken up with the process? Do they not realize it is not *you* who goes—but you are the process?

If your life has been well-lived, you are free to choose if you wish to return, but do not choose it this time. The work of this world is over! You must begin to be You and advance to the next plane. The work of Earth is such that it will take too many years to be able to change all the terrible things done to it, thus we want you out of here!

Today's class is one of survival. You are to survive, but not by your wits. You are to survive because you are *you* and know why *you* are You. If that lesson is lost, you are lost.

So ends this lesson.

Chapter Four

The world is not here!

The World exists within each of you, and if you desire to change it, you do. It is not nearly as complicated as certain philosophers have described. It is a simple mechanism that permits you to explore different aspects of the human condition.

The many ways you are can be explored, but only one at a time. This is why so many get off track. Some want to explore one facet of personality, while others seek a different route. This leads some to drop their original quest—which then confuses the rest. You must stick to your own quest if you are to resolve your life issues.

If your work of spirit is not great, you are unable to grow. You may develop into a known human (famous person) of great wealth, but the real *you* did not develop. This is a waste of a life.

No matter how much money you may have, do you know who *you* are? Within wealth is a barrier. You must not let wealth be a goal. It is a sub-goal. You reach for the worth of *you*, and it comes along with it. Many who are poor are not much better off than the wealthy. You must not let wealth or lack thereof become a reason for not sincerely seeking to be all you are meant to be.

The reason you stop seeking has no bearing on the life you chose. The reason is—you chose not to seek. Many choose not to be wealthy! You are surprised? Why?

If wealth was the reason you were here, then it would be a very happy time for all who attained it, but usually it is not. If your wealth constricts your activities, making it difficult for you to circulate among others, you are not free. You are imprisoned by it. You must give enough away, so you have plenty for your needs, but not enough to keep you out of circulation. If the work of God is not enough to clothe or feed you, then you will give away too much. God gives all enough.

We seek to help you understand the underpinnings of this world—which your people in the past negotiated. It is not a world we particularly approve of now, but it is not our place to criticize it. We are here to teach you ways that enable you to enter the next plane when you cross over from this one. We do not want you to be upset. We want you to be there!

In the beginning of this work you asked for help. Did you remember to thank God then? You must never ask God or anyone for a favor and not thank them in advance. It is not proper and lacks good manners. So what, you say? Well, it is the truth. You are all too close in time and space to exist easily without manners or a code of ethics.

THE WORK BEGINS

You must live as one,
You must learn that
The way of The World is—
Blend in or die!

To die in The World is not the same as dying. To die in the world refers to those who are no longer considered to be a part of their society. They are not respected. They are socially unacceptable. They are ignored by those most responsible for the good life in that society. A life of crime will most assuredly deaden you to a life in this society.

A life lived among those who strive to enrich the work of this world enables you to grow and be accepted, but not if you decide to break the common rules of etiquette. You cannot ignore them! They will ruin your chances for success if you do.

If you die in this world, you could move to another area or society and begin again, but few do. Most people who drop out go to another area where they feel more comfortable. Prisons are colonies of ex-citizens who are ousted and told to learn better manners. If they do that, they may work back into society, but it takes time. If they refuse, they will be back in prison again. This is a very simple example, but it is sufficient.

Now if you are flirting with the idea of being different—and most of you are—we suggest you control that urge. The main reason Earth has been destroyed is because you all wanted to be rich. No one wanted to be poor. Next, you decided it was better to be rich and not work, so you left the work of Earth and entered into handling ideas. This is the stage in life where you no longer work with your hands, but use your mind.

We are not averse to you using your mind, but you must use your hands, too. A person who uses only the mind is incapable of implementing its ideas, but a person who uses both hands and mind can. It is not a difficult decision to make. Use both to circumvent the rules of society and you are viewed as both an individual and a success, otherwise—no way.

When you are free, you feel fear leave. But as long as you experience any form of fear, you know you are not free. To be free is the effort of being *you*. You can understand it, but it is not tangible. You know it, but it cannot be described. The feeling of freedom is the greatest known feeling on the plane where you reside now. You must strive to feel it at least once.

The efforts of many are often directed at controlling the lives of others. We see threats and counter threats every day and marvel at the ability of some to concentrate their energy on just one person whom they wish to annihilate. Since that person has Spiritual Guides protecting and watching for such attacks, what do you think happens to the person perpetuating such viciousness? You can only wonder at the ego of people who believe they can cross the wards of God's holy helpers. You must never try to learn that lesson! But if you already have, you know life is not nearly as good as it was before you attempted to control or destroy another.

THE WORK BEGINS

The work of your mind is tangible, but not to you. We see the manifestations of your minds, but make no move to change them. If you do, your thoughts will be blocked. If you have a great idea and are determined to make it happen now, we suggest you concentrate solely upon it and not be disturbed by any chance occurrences that appear to say it cannot be. If against all odds you can concentrate, you can achieve your dream. No big deal!

If a student is ready for the next step, the teacher is already there or another appears. If the student requires different material, it may appear in the form of words spoken by another entity from another area of life, but the material is always there. The student is not asked to bring paper or pencil, but good students are always prepared. If you wish to bring along all you know, you may be told you are not interested in changing, but that is not a big problem.

You must sort through past ideas from time-to-time and discard those that are not appropriate to the life you choose to live now. If the stories of youth are silly or inane, drop them. Do not sit and ask questions of the teacher—listen instead. Your own mind can answer questions. You need only think the question and the teacher will answer it right away, so be quiet within and let those wiser than you talk.

Many times in life you find yourself called upon to teach. If you shirk this responsibility, you do not grow. You must never shirk work. The end of the line is the day you refuse to grow, then you are unable to continue and might as well be dead.

Teachers grow, but students are more able to grow. Do not stop the progress of a soul.

In the work of your world are many opportunities to grow, but so much is now destroyed. Men and women are seeking to be established and seen as great mentors, but are they? We see few men and women helping anyone to succeed in the workplace. You will be asked to help, and if you do not, you will be held responsible for it. No one can turn down a plea for help and live a full life. You will be diminished by the degree of help you failed to give. If you help, your life is extended beyond the length of time you requested before coming to this plane.

Another way to extend your life beyond the time predestined is to act with protectiveness toward all who cannot be strong. The weak need the strong to keep the world safe for them. If you permit the trafficking of drugs, guns, and other violent means to end life, you will be held responsible for any evil outcomes. The work of this world is not evil, but good. Swift work is made of those who cannot do good work. It is no problem to send them back again to relive this life.

Yet another way to extend life is to honor and uphold the visions of your parents. You may not agree with their ways, but they did agree to enlarge you and help you grow. If they have done all they can—maybe not as much as some would wish—you owe them respect for helping you become whoever you are. You must never forsake them or ignore their needs. If you do, you will not have enough time to do your work and will have to return. If you honor them all their days, your life is long enough to do whatever you chose to do at birth.

We expect to be respected, but we are not of your plane and cannot exert any pressure upon you to do so. If you cannot respect your parents, it is impossible for you to respect us. We will not be interested in how much you advance. You will have to live life your own way.

In the work of your world are many who work with people who upset them and cause them to fear. This is not to continue. The world must be rid of such artificial work. The work of The Holy Spirit is not to be subverted. It is not to be used to advance evil. You will all pay for using others' work to destroy Earth. You are held responsible if you continue to do it. We are not the ones to condemn, but we know the rules.

You are not the only beings on Earth, but you are in control. The others exist on another plane and in another world, but they exist. If you doubt it, ask your Spiritual Guides to help you explore that realm. It is often in your dreams. We will teach nothing of that realm, since it has no bearing on *you*, but such work is not to be destroyed.

We are unable to understand why you do not like to be on the air. You talk on the telephone, and always ask to be rich and famous, but if asked to address the public, you hate it. How can you be *you* if you do not know how to communicate? We seek those who do like to communicate and ask them to help us. You, too, will be asked to help if your life has been one of dedicated work and you can communicate.

If you doubt the work of another, it may be because you do not know the complexity of their job. If you shirk your work, all know you are not ready for advancement. You are not to advance in the work of Spirit if you shirk meditation. It is not easy work, but it is absolutely necessary! You cannot listen to God if you cannot remain silent.

If the work of God is not the work of You, we will not bother to continue talking about it. We sense the work of some people who hear us is not the work of God—but it could be. We strongly urge you to change whatever keeps you from doing the work of God, and correct your attitude.

Devil worshippers are not worshipping a devil. You must know that, yet some fear it. The work of such cults is not a device to gain knowledge—but to gain power. Such power is not to be given to them! You may not be aware of it, but they will short-circuit their lives. You need not fear anyone who claims to be a warlock or witch, because such idiotic titles are just that. We seek sincere people to help now—no such individuals need apply.

The Church has promoted the belief in the power of evil, but God does not care. It is a means to an end, but not a good way to teach. Fear is never the best way to teach, but for some it has its place. We notice some look at all channeled material in the hopes of finding something that can be termed as *evil*. Why? Are you so pure of spirit you can be a judge of such work? That is difficult to believe!

The means to the end is not to be wasted on idle work of Spirit now, and *you* must concern yourself with saving *you*. We do not want more energy spent exploring psychic development or any other such ideas, because you will develop psychically if you meditate. It is the automatic result of listening to God.

The work of God is never at the root of anyone's problems, but the work of man usually is. You need to sort through the world's work and find what is best for you to do—then do it. If you do not find a job that encourages you, change it; but if you continually change jobs, you are the one at fault—you are not at peace and must meditate more.

The work of The World is an occupation of the mind and hands that enables you to grow spiritually—and must occur. If you do no work, you do not grow. Your strength is sapped and you wither. This is not the way to end a life.

You must continue to work even if The World said you are not wanted. You have to work in order to remain alive. If you stop working, you will be unable to continue long on Earth. If you no longer have to work to feed and clothe you and your responsibilities, devise a means whereby you can gain access into the mind and heart of You, so you can sort through the reasons given for you to live this time.

If you choose to write, write—but not about you. No one is interested in another life story. These times are perilous. You must write of what may help The World change and persevere, not write about your accomplishments in a time that no longer exists. People read stories of greatness in order to gain insight into how that person could rise above The World and live as he or she wished, but few books ever scale such heights—most are recitals of achievements no longer remembered by The World. You must do all you can to improve The World. Recalling your life has little to do with that.

Whatever you read, be sure it is worthwhile. The mind is a blank space filled by whatever you read or look at. If you fill your mind with terror and violence, it is repeated over and over again until it no longer has any effect. You become numb to it. To fill your eyes with beauty is the same as living in beauty.

You must seek contrast!

Whatever you see now is not The World's work, but the work of one person. One person originally had an idea and that idea was expanded upon until it now exists and appears to be a large man-made monument, but it is not. It is merely the vision of one person. You can erect anything you sincerely wish to build, but it is your faith that creates it—not the work of others.

People help people achieve their dreams. That is how the world of work was created, but today all the dreamers are gone. Those left are in search of fame and money. If today's news is good, no one cares if the news of tomorrow will be bad.

You look back not forward—
But the past is gone!

When you seek fame and fortune, you are not seeking God. You may think you are, but you are not. We seek out those who are humble and meek, but not always. Many have sought fame and money and found it to be of no use, thus are welcome to move to the front of the class now. We need you to explain to others that life is not made of money.

If your life is an example of what not to do, we suggest you clearly identify that to others before you start preaching. Many say so much about their evil days that one can almost see their pride in it. We suggest you sign off if the speaker has nothing to say but how he or she became famous. This is of no use to *you*. You should curb your appetite for knowledge of the inner lives of others. You have to live your life, and such involvement is not conducive to your further enrichment. In fact, it could give you the wrong impression.

Today the work of communications people is to encourage the wanton fantasies of the work force, so its labor continues. They hold themselves above such trivial work, but continue to produce it. Only today's media can reach many people who need to be taught now.

If you do not do it, who will? Most of The World can decide if it needs you, but some are starved for information. Are you giving people the best you know? Are you helping others? Are you delivering the message that helped you become the person you are today?

We strongly urge all in the world of communications to view their work and correct its direction, if it is not moving toward the light of God. You know it, so change it. Your ability to transcend The World in a single sentence is not to be idly used. If you answer the needs of the people, you will be rich and famous—we can guarantee that! If you do not, you will answer for it at the end of this life. You have been chosen, be sure you deserve it.

The movies of today are no different than in the past, but you are. You no longer fear images that once scared you, but they scare others who are as familiar with images of the past as you are. You must be held responsible for overindulging the wantonness of those who have money to expound their perverted dreams. If you do not censor your work, who will? We will!

We are about to change all—and you will be left behind. You do not reach anyone now, but you do not know it yet. The day of teenage manipulation has had its effect, and The World is aware of the power of images and sounds, but you are not. It will defeat *you* if you do not change. No amount of money can earn *you* a place among the dead who transcend this plane. It is only the work of God that earns that privilege. If you can, stop and redirect. If you cannot, we will see you here on Earth again.

The many movies you produce are like the movie of your life. You cannot be *you* if you do not write a script, select a role, and induce others to co-star with you—then you need costumes and props to decorate the scenes of your life. It is all you. You are even the clothes you wear. You are always seen as being the work of *you*. If you look as though a ragman dressed you, you are not rich in the eyes of everyone else—even if you are.

The World is not as idle as it once was, but it is far from busy. Many people do very little. Instead, they sit and plot. Is that work? No! Idleness is what we abhor—not time spent doing nothing. There is a big difference.

To meditate requires you to settle down and listen to the words of God within you. You cannot do that easily if you do not achieve stillness and silence. Once you are adept, you can live in meditation. We seek those who do, but first you must stop, look within, and then listen to the words of God.

We will end now. You are to begin the next session after a period of meditation. If you do not meditate, it will not make sense to *you*.

Chapter Five

The work of this day is to determine if you will be able to deliver the goods at the end of this life. Will you be there with a lot of work done—or with much unfinished business that results in your being returned to Earth for another try? The examination is not stringent, but it is relentless.

Certain criteria must be met in each life, regardless of why you returned now—and if not met, you cannot be promoted to the next plane. We will not belabor what was written in the previous volume (*We Are Here*), nor do we intend to repeat things as many times as we did in that book, since it is the primer, but you may not have fully comprehended its contents yet or have not read it, so we repeat this lesson—but only once.

If the world is not for you and you wish to live on the next plane, you must:

1. Do no evil to anyone. This means everyone—including you. If you call names or gossip about others; if you spare no one any pain or suffering—in fact, inflict it; if you are selfish and determined to always have your way; if you let no one ever listen in peace to the word of God; if you cause others to fear you; if you kill or rape; if you scorn what is godly; if you call upon the name of God in

the presence of others to scoff; if you care not for your children when young, or parents in old age; if you feel only you count in this world and act accordingly; if you are unwilling to help others. Each of these things is bad in and of itself, but combine them and you place your soul in what you call *mortal jeopardy*, which can result in the decision going against you at the end and causing *you* to be returned to Earth. If you intentionally kill another human being, kill yourself, or blasphemy God—it results in two returns to Earth. You are a creation of God. You must honor God!

2. The work of this world was given to you to do. If you do no work, you are not doing your share. You must learn that lesson or come back and do more the next time. If you work hard every day, you can at least assure yourself you will not have to work as hard if you do come back.

3. You must learn to tolerate all human beings. The work of The World is not the same as on higher planes, but souls are. If you cannot learn to get along on Earth, you will be forced to conform to a set of rules so stringent it is easier to return here than go forward. If this is the last time you can be on Earth, you will be hampered in *your future*.

This world is not the only world, nor is this the only place you live now. You live within a multi-dimensional being and reside in more than one location at a time. Actually, time and space are nonexistent, except in the minds of humans. You have built this universe in order to explain your existence, but it does not really exist.

Since you feel insignificant, you like to break everything down and explain it. We of the upper planes are not interested in stories and plots you make up, but we are concerned if such tales lead souls astray. The worst of your stories is the one about *science*. We sense many do not believe it, but are intimidated into saying they do. The only way to avoid ignorance such as this is to teach the truth. We will begin to teach the way of God, and if that frightens you, we have accomplished something.

Never sit and destroy the dreams of another! You are in effect taking away their life. If you destroy a dream, which is another aspect of a personality exploring this universe, it cannot continue and results in stunted growth. We encourage exploration on all planes as a human, but it results in no real growth. You must enter the upper regions before growth takes place, but practicing while confined to Earth is not a bad way to prepare oneself.

In the event you are not confined to Earth—actually you float quite freely above *you* at times, we congratulate you on being able to outlast criticism and destroy the motives of those who would hold you prisoner. If you cannot flee Earth, you will be confined here to the end—and the end is nearing at an alarming rate.

We never anticipated that Earth could be destroyed. It was the decision of a select few who destroyed and looted all Earth's minerals and fluids in order to gain control of money. No power is assured them, such is the way of selfish people.

If Earth were to die tomorrow, could you fly away? No, you are of Earth. You would be present to see the last moments, but it would not be *your* last moment. If you could not advance then, you would be vaporized and returned to the state previous to this one.

We are here to help you advance to a higher plane rather than return to a lower one. What would happen if you dropped a level? You would prefer not to know. We are here to help—not scare you into submission.

If the work of this world is not of your mind, why are you here? This is the time to be *you*—to enjoy the privilege of existing in flesh and interacting with others who will share your life on the planes above. If you jealously guard all you have, you will find reluctance on the part of others to share their secrets, too. If you share knowledge, you can call upon others for help.

Sharing is now a serious problem on Earth. It never existed in prior times, but today in your time it is the norm to not help each other. You must make this easy change.

If the work of this world is not in your mind, why do you care? This is the time you are *you*. You are here to learn to deal with negativity and flesh. You are confined here to movement in only a few dimensions, but you are still aware of the past and probable future of your actions while here. We suggest you forget the past and probable outcomes in order to concentrate on living in the NOW. You will then have a good tomorrow.

THE WORK BEGINS

In the work of your hands is much that soothes the spirit, so you must do it. If you sit and read and never write, what do you gain? You cannot communicate. You selfishly ignore the output you could make that would help the rest fully understand the reason they are here.

If philosophers are not born but made, who do you think you are now? You are the only philosopher to be born in your time and place, so you can philosophize. It is the right of the mature to tell the young what they think or believe. If the young do not understand, the mature must explain while not denying the young the opportunity to pursue their own wisdom. If you refuse to exact the respect required to give wisdom, you are the fool—not the youth.

When the work of your hands is unfulfilling, you cannot connect to The Holy Spirit through it. It is not a deep, profound thing. It is simply a fact that you like to touch. You like to feel. You feel it is better to be involved in something than sit back and watch. These thoughts cause you to believe in the work of the mind, but you do not enjoy it, thus you never give up handwork. It is of the Earth.

Your own life is not the life of another, nor can another do your work. You cannot be expected to do their work, nor expect someone to do yours, but too many people expect that now. We condone The World's denial of goods to those who refuse to work in a manner conducive to prospering in this world. If you cannot make a living one way, try another, and another until you find one. If you always experience difficulties, you are either not trying or not working.

This is not a difficult world! You created it and placed obstacles in your path in order to get as much out of this experience as possible. If we remove them, you will be less motivated to pursue the truth.

There is much in the work of the next plane that is unknown to you, but much is similar to this work. You must work constantly there, too. If you are not in the habit of working, you will be held in a special area until you establish the routine necessary to do that work. You can learn it while here on Earth.

Some of you blame, blame, blame. You think others are responsible for you. You are wrong! You, alone, are responsible for all that is and all there will be in your life. If the world has changed since you entered it, you as an intelligent being who knew other times here have the opportunity to explore and investigate. If your experience is such that you can lend light to the present, you should.

We are not interested in people showing off. We want you to be *you*, but remember all others have to be themselves, too. This is why too many have difficulties today. They see the need to be themselves but believe it is their responsibility to share what they know with only a select few. This is the behavior of those who upon entering the next plane will be shipped to the outer areas and not incorporated into the whole immediately.

In each heart is a space reserved for the past. It is in this space where you store memories. We suggest you root through them from time-to-time and release agony and pretend instead to exist only in love. It is a harmless exercise. It causes no one pain, but releases energy for further use. You will feel sorrow fly from you. Let it go!

In each mind there exists a place where you make plans for the future. If you do not, it is a hair-raising ride through this life, but not all bad. If you overload the mind, you are perpetually worrying. This is the fault of a mind with no outlet. You need to work on plans stored in your mind. You also need to free yourself of worry.

If only you could be *you*, we would have no reason to be here. If only you could say, "I will be all I came here to be," we could leave. We have been here only a short time and see the work is long-term. We expect to be here for a long time, but not forever.

We are not to enter your life or control you, but you will feel our presence. We intend to monitor your progress. You alone are the one we want. We do not care if none of your family or friends wants to go forward. We care only if you want to move ahead at the end of this life.

We are not the only ones on Earth to be sent by God, but we are the only teachers. If you need help, you need only ask, but this work is for you alone to do. You cannot say you had no help here. You have all the help you need—always. If you steadfastly refuse to ask, you are a fool.

The work of the next plane is not for fools, so you will not be encouraged to seek it at the end of this life. We review all that is and are unconcerned because you lacked instruction in the past. In the future you cannot say schooling was unavailable to take classes and learn from the work of God what was necessary to insure you would advance to the next life at the end of this one.

The work of this session is now over. We have carried you forward. We have told you much. We are tired of talk. You now must learn for yourself.

The next assignment is an attempt to understand why you insist on staying behind—life-after-life. Do you think it is good work for your soul to stay here? It is not! Do you think it is the only work of your soul? It is not! You are here to advance to the next plane.

You are not here to spend your eternal soul's life on a lower plane. You are meant to fulfill the entire, enormous capability of You, and go forward to the next area where *you* learn more and advance. If you stay here, you cannot go on to the great life. You are stuck. We will help you get out of the rut you are in and advance. We will aim our work at doing this now.

This is the time to begin a journal of the work of your soul. You could write it out or keep it in your mind, but writing with the hand and mind soothes *you*. We suggest you begin to write now. If your handwork is not smooth, we will help you. We inspire, but never actually write.

Guides are known to write through you, but not us. We are only here to help you progress. We are not here to preen and care for your soul. You will be held up to the light and examined, but it is not our work that will cause you to drop from the roster of those who advance. It is the work of *you* and *your* Guides. You are who must work to clear the air now.

If writing words is too difficult—draw. Pick up a piece of charcoal, a crayon, or paint and draw—just do it! You cannot tell someone else to draw for you. You alone see the picture. You alone see the image of *you*. If your pictures are difficult to interpret, we suggest you limit yourself to only one, until it becomes clear to you. To continue in a state of disturbance is unwise. It does nothing for *you*.

This is the last time we will enter into the discussion of why you are here and why you must listen.

Chapter Six

The work of this world is not to be here and then disappear. It is to do what you came here to do, and if it is satisfactory, to be elevated to the next plane. You often say you know you have something to do while here, but do not know what it is. We are telling you what it is now.

You are here to do the work of *you*, not the work of this world as it is, but work as you decided it would be. If you do not like this work once on Earth, you need only change it and have your plan reviewed. Once the new plan is reviewed and accepted by the High Guide, you can proceed to work on it; however, if your plan is selfish and otherwise unacceptable, you will be told to try again or return to the original plan.

In life you will feel spiritual constraints, but may not recognize them. You may start out on the wrong foot and end up in the wrong area of work. It will not enable you to concentrate on your work of The Holy Spirit. If this happens, you are made to feel so uncomfortable that *you* change.

We suggest you always pray before beginning a new project. If the answer is not there, then try another time. We see so few of you go into prayer and most cannot meditate.

If you cannot meditate, you cannot be in touch with You. It is that simple. Once you are out of touch with You, you are out of touch with your own reality. You are a known quantity—but seldom understood. You must seek to be *you*. If you have trouble doing this, you are in trouble.

This is the time to seek the real personality who lies within your human body. If the real *you* is absent, you have to coax You to return and remove the shackles imprisoning *you*. If the chains that bind you are of your own making, remove them. If they are forged over time and involve many others, you will require help. This help is always available, but requires prayer. You must guarantee others they will not be hurt. If you can do that, you can free yourself. If you cannot devise a way out of your troubles that will not harm another, you are told to try another life. This is when a *walk-in* is often offered the job. You know if that happens.

Walk-ins are not like you, but are of You. They reside within the framework of the soul, but have not lived on Earth. You are the only one on Earth. No one else within You can enter the Earth plane as long as one aspect of the personality is here; but if the one on Earth cannot achieve much, another aspect may be sent to take its place.

To many humans now, there are many areas of doubt and uncertainty in the work of the multi-dimensional soul, but not to us. We can answer all of these questions in due course—once the main work is done. If you have to ask questions, you must be prepared to listen. So many humans ask questions now but never listen to the answers. We hear a million cries, but only a few meditate today. If it is the intent of *you* to be free of Earth, why not prepare for the next step?

We are not of Earth, but it is not that complex. It is not as difficult to work on Earth as you try to make it out now. If you have it so bad, why do so many people stay here for so many lives? We are not unimpressed by the stories of treachery and deceit that abound, nor do we intend to help those who use such tactics. We will help only those who can advance the work of God.

In the world of your making are few who understand it, but The World is not that big. You will have great difficulty in the next world if you cannot understand the one you are in now. We suggest you return to studying the world—not sitting and staring at the tube of renown (television). You need stimulation, but it is not present there. We will help you break down the need to be entertained and return to your work.

If you begin each day with prayer, you feel better. You look relaxed and intent—eager for the new day. If you sit and stare at a television in your room, you appear to be asleep. You look like you are not awake to the fact that life is within *you*—not out there somewhere.

In the world of today are many distractions, but few are worthy of you. You sit and watch—staring, not moving a muscle. Is this the work of the body, mind, or spirit? We think none are involved. Why not move? Why not get into the action? Why sit and watch others having fun and living now?

Once you decide to be *you*, we cannot predict the area in which you will excel, but you definitely do a lot better than when you sit and watch others excel.

If your work is too easy—and it is now for most Americans, Europeans, and Arabs—you will see the world is not fit for the rest. You have a responsibility to do more. You are to do the only thing you know. You must do it well and do it often.

If you do not work, you will be unable to do the work of Spirit. If the work of Spirit is not done, you are faced with being returned to another plane. It may no longer be an option to return to Earth. You may be sent to a plane where life is quite difficult and confining. Although it has been traversed before, it will be the only opening available.

You should avoid having to return

If your work is not done and now sits, we will help, but you must also work. The only one to sit and then advance was Buddha. He taught. You do not teach others by sitting. You are not a Buddha. Yogis are advanced souls, but they work. You are the only ones to sit and do nothing. Is that the way of advancement? You know that in your work world sitting would result in dismissal, so why would it be acceptable in the work of your spiritual life?

When the soul seeks wisdom and light, the mind is free. If the mind is busy on its work, the body is free. If the body is busy, soul and mind are free. This is the most efficient way to free *you*.

Let us go forth and seek other means to effectively change your way of life in order to advance you on this plane. In this plane are many different places where you can advance into elsewhere, but few are available. If you want to advance, you must work.

If your work is acceptable, you may be permitted to advance on this plane to a higher level. We accept you as equal to those already there, but it is extremely difficult. It is as difficult to accomplish this, as it is to advance socially on this world level. Usually you cannot enter life in one social order and advance to another. Usually women are permitted such advancement, but men seldom are allowed. If you do the work required, you may be asked to move up, but you cannot make it happen.

In the work of this world are a few inconsistencies, but none exist in the work of the soul. You may not realize you lie every day, but all of you do. You constantly seek the less adventurous life. You never ask for what you want. You always complain. You ask others to do things you do not want them to do, and ask others to do your work. Are these the traits of a winning personality? They are on Earth! In the planes above, these traits will result in demotion.

If the work of this world is not wonderful, why are we asking you to do it? Because it is the work of this world! You must do what you are told. If you deny the right to be *you*, you deny God. Many are not trying to establish a pathway—let alone live. If you have no route to the top mapped out, how do you expect to get there? We can see few are aware of the top, let alone aware it may be easily achieved. We are amazed!

If your work exhausts you, you are not planning your day. You cannot be exhausted if you know where and when to end your labor and begin your own work. If this is a problem for you, begin keeping a journal and writing in it the last thing before going to bed. Once you know where you left off, you can begin there the next day.

If the work you did was trivial, it will set off alarm bells indicating you are wasting valuable time. If your work is worthwhile—and it should be, you will see a day or two go by without movement, then a day of movement, and then a lapse of time and all is done. You were not moving constantly, but the work was. You were materializing the ideas.

You need time to let work grow and develop

If you act upon each idea as it comes to you, success is easier to achieve. If you let ideas accumulate, you have to sort out what you prefer—and thus lose time. If you act immediately, you have many ideas and achieve much. The few on Earth who do this are multi-millionaires, while the rest are still trying to get started.

If the work of each day is incomplete, you are unable to go forward. You must first finish that day's work. Do not try to start another project then or both will fail. You need to concentrate. If you do not, you cannot imagine the final outcome. If you cannot *see* it as done, you will not see it done. You have to visualize. If time for visualization is not used, the project is worse for it. You need time, but you waste it now. That time of life you always talk about is *now*!

When the work of your day is finished, you may sit and enjoy the *you* whom you know in this world; but before you sit, meditate and let us ask you questions about the next day, so we can begin it for you. When this is done, you are free of your mind. You can do whatever you wish. You can make the work of your mind, body, or soul disappear, or you can stare into the tube in your room. It is okay to do it then.

We are not afraid of the tube. It is not a television, rather a mechanism that channels. We seek the transmission of ideas and facts. We seek someone to tell you how to be on the right track, but we seek others as well. If you can do this, you may apply.

Whatever you do, do it with the verve of an outstanding person and it will be well received by the world. In this world you have several mechanisms built-in: fame, money, full-time employment for idlers, advanced education for idiots, and a lot of frivolous ideas, but the real test of any society is its output. How many are truly educated? How many are poor? How many live well today? If the society is doing great, the answers are reflected in the numbers.

When you cannot work, you cannot contribute. But when are you unable to work? Can you work if you have been physically injured? Of course, you can work! Your mind is fine and your soul is intact.

If you are considered to be insane, you may not be working in this world, but still working on this plane. You are to work until the body is gone. Once the body is gone, you pass on to the next plane—if you worked hard and hurt no one along the way.

～

What is the work of this world?
You are the world—you decide!

We are not here to assign tasks or get involved in the management of assets. You are responsible and cannot blame us for your lack of interest. You will be asked to pay, because you alone destroyed Earth. No other beings on Earth have done damage to its surface. You are the greedy ones.

The work of God is being preached now, but not lived. We want you to live the work of God and not preach. Is this too difficult?

We are angry that so many are unable to pay for what they buy. That is greed! If you buy a necessity, you were given the money. We know. The needs of Earth are always met, but not all the wants. If your wants exceed your money, you are greedy if you continue to make demands. If your wants are met, you are the most fortunate of beings. We commend you for knowing how to manipulate The World to your advantage.

If your work is not as desirable as what some do, you are paid more to do it. If the amount paid is the criteria for how much others respect you, why get down on you? Do the job you are paid to do. You are responsible for how The World treats you.

In this world there are many who try to deny they are responsible for the life they live. No one believes them. No one will ever believe them. So why do you whine? Whiners are losers. It is that simple. You do not have to cry, but some believe it is the best or only way to get their way. Whiners are disliked by others. We want you to face justice when you have done wrong. Sit up and take it, and do not act up and carry on if you made a mistake. You learn so much from a mistake that later it is not regarded as a mistake.

Once the work of your life is done, your work is reviewed and criticized. You are given a chance to explain why you did it as you did, but no one can explain a lack of remorse for doing wrong. You are unable to say: '*I did it and I do not care.*' If you do say that, it is back to Earth for *you!* For our sake, do not say it. We are here to get you to the next plane. We do not want you returned at the end.

If you are unable to compensate a victim, why let the one who did the damage go unscathed? In the past some have created a false set of values and others continue to accept them even now. You, as a group, must change such injustices. It is your society, so make changes. Whenever an injustice is allowed to continue, you are all held accountable. If the one who is wrong has to pay, all of you should be compensated for it.

The work of the soul is not the only way to move up in the world, but it is the best way. You are aware only of the body's work, but the soul is the greater part of your work here. You are not the only one who cares about *you*, but you are the only one held responsible.

If the work of your day is done, and you have not done work on self, you are not done working yet. You need to meditate. You need to learn from within what you lack. You need to delve into the recesses of your mind and develop the best way to do your work—both of body and mind. Once you know the best way to proceed, you are ready to be *you*. If *you* are done working with You, you may do whatever you wish for the rest of the day.

In The World there are many who will not like you if you tell them to work—yet you do. You tell people to work when you refuse to give them assets you developed or money. You can stop much needless waste by refusing to be a part of it.

It is not necessary to run around talking,
But it is necessary to work!

Others notice if you are a success. It is not necessary to spend money telling people you are. Truly, the only one who cares if you are a success is *you*. All others are merely interested. You care if you fail, so why cater to others? Why not be *you*? Is it so strange? Of course, it is not!

You can use sense to live your life, but not to think. When you sit back and rest, most let your ego go wild. It is so out of control that some never hear the Higher Self speak. You never know if the move you are about to make is good or not. You cannot hear anything but static. If you wish, this ends today. You need only begin to meditate.

Meditation is the key to all soul searching

If you insist you cannot meditate, you are announcing you are incapable of being in charge. If a person cannot control the ego, how can that person be a good manager? No way can it happen! You must first control that which is within you—then you can think about controlling others. Most people are eager to control all others first—then meditate. It does not work that way. We are here to tell you that you cannot be in charge of anyone else if you are out of touch with You.

In the work of the world are many ways to avoid labor, but few are recognized. In the workplace there are those who never work. They are there to *manage* others. What a laugh! You laugh, too. It is not so obvious though to those who pay them. Why would you pay someone to sit and tell others to work? You are not slave masters.

You are the product of many universities and, although education is not as elevated as it should be, it is still good. So why would you sit and stare and do very little? You need to work, too. You need to produce. You need to feel you are there for a purpose. If you do not work, you will be unhappy.

Once the work of The World sours, it is not long until you are out of work, but you need to work for *you*. You are not to sit and stare or worry. If work worries you, maybe you are not suited to do it? If the work makes you unhappy, maybe you are not there for the right reason? If you are happy and productive, why change your work?

Many people seek higher jobs even though they are content where they are. This is greed. You will not be pleased by a higher position. You will learn, because it is a lesson you will remember. We see you learn best when you have problems, so we will pretend to be you and ask how you should do things.

PROBLEM: You are in the workplace and hear someone tell another they intend to steal something. You wonder what you should do.

ANSWER: You are in serious trouble if this is a problem. We want you to know instantly what to do. In this situation rise immediately and enter the conversation. Once you hear what is proposed, tell both involved that it is a bad idea, which ends your participation.

PROBLEM: You work while many others shirk their work, and you feel you may get into trouble with them for working too hard.

ANSWER: You have no problem until you start slowing down.

PROBLEM: You are at work and your supervisor cannot show you what to do. Your supervisor is furious that you do not know and ask repeatedly for help. You now feel you might lose your job if you ask again. Should you talk to the supervisor's superior or will you be fired for doing that?

ANSWER: If your supervisor cannot supervise, you have the right to go higher. But if you go higher in order to embarrass your boss, you will be put down or fired. Never go over the head of someone above you unless there is no other way.

PROBLEM: You believe all the pretty women are being promoted, so you decide to change your appearance. Is this the best way to get ahead?

ANSWER: The world recognizes beauty, but does not pay for it. You need to develop other aspects of *you* that command money if that is what you seek. You are not to alter your body. God created it and expects you to keep it in good shape. To alter it suggests it is not good enough for you—which is not the way to please anyone.

PROBLEM: You are injured and cannot work as well as usual. Should you complain or work less?

ANSWER: An injury is a temporary condition, but the job is permanent. You must establish lines of communication that support you in such times. If you are trustworthy, no one will doubt you are not feeling well; but if you are a liar, you can expect to be doubted when you report problems.

PROBLEM: You seek a job where there are no others like you. Would it be wise to call their attention to this?

ANSWER: Not if you really want to work. You are to seek work—not seek trouble. If your work is good, you will be hired eventually—if not there, somewhere else. You must avoid the possibility of developing a poor attitude and causing needless grief for yourself. The work of the world is not *you*. It is merely the means of raising your living standard. You can live off the land, but few today wish to do it.

PROBLEM: Your work is less and less interesting. You feel it could be better, but the boss is not interested in your ideas. What should you do?

ANSWER: We suggest—and it is merely a suggestion—that all who find themselves feeling like this should draw up a list of ways the new idea would improve the final product or save money for the company. Use figures since business uses figures to make decisions. In your personal life, however, figures are usually abandoned, because they do not help much.

PROBLEM: You sit and watch others act the fool and prance around after the boss. Should you do it, too?

ANSWER: Your life is your life. If you are to be the court jester, you could do worse; but if you want to be a star, you would hinder your chances by doing that. We suggest you decide which role suits you. Obviously, the intelligent boss is not fooled; but how many intelligent supervisors are there?

We listed a few areas of worry for many of you, but you will have more and more questions, and no one can answer all of *your* worries—but You. You have all the answers within You. You only have to know how to access them.

By the way, the answer is: **MEDITATE**

If we continue to harp on this subject, it is because some students are dense and refuse to acknowledge this as the only way to get ahead today.

We will drop this lesson now in order to examine you to see if it registered. You do know we can see you. Even if you are not at home or on the job, you are always working on *you*. Begin now to make this the best time of your life. We will be back.

Chapter Seven

The day's work is to be over and done by the time the sun sets. If the sun sets long after hours, you continue to work at home. The end of a day is not the end of the time you work on self; it is the time when you put aside other worldly matters to concentrate solely on *you*.

The end of The World you live in now is not the same as the end of Earth. It is entirely different. You chose to build a life of work. You chose to end each day at sundown. You chose to build the work of man into monuments to such effort.

We are not here to criticize the idea or the means by which you fill time from birth to death. It is not the way of God to inform you of your mistakes. It is, however, time to begin to understand these are *your* mistakes.

If you seek your Lord in all you do, do you think you will find him? We doubt that you care. You work, because it is what you do, but it is *only* a means for you to earn a living. What if you could do whatever you chose to do? What if this life was the only one you had and you are required to finish now all you started out to do?

Actually, this is the only life you have now. It is one more episode called life while you are on Earth. You often refer to *past lives* as though you died and were reborn. This is in error and should be corrected. You are *you* only—and You do not die!

After the creation of your being, you could direct your energy in a number of different directions, but all here chose to come to Earth. It is not the easiest place in which to pursue God, but it accounts for a large number of beings. You will know more about this later, now we are concentrating on why you need to work.

In the beginning of your time, which is not the beginning of time on Earth, you decided to build a new kind of world. You destroyed all traces of the old world in order to build your own. You wanted nothing left to remind some people of the old ways, but many decided to preserve them anyway. If you cannot understand this, you must begin to study ancient history. We do not have time to develop what has already been taught.

If the books you read are inaccurate, we will point out errors—otherwise read, and read, and read. It is the point you take, not the direction of the material. Whenever the material you read is not direct or is inaccurate, you can feel it in the touch of the page and know it, yet not know where it is inaccurate. We can enter your mind and develop the theme so you may reenter those times and relive them again. It is a very entertaining way to relearn the old ways. Now let up on history and begin again working on today.

THE WORK BEGINS

*If the world is imperfect,
It is your fault—not God's*

We often hear people mourning at gravesites blaming God for whatever. How can this be? How can God enter into your life and snatch away what you were preparing to let die? You must recognize it is the decision of those far more advanced than you that Earth is a classroom and not the destination of your soul. Your soul is not to be condemned to Earth.

You are not the only ones here, but the rest do not blame God. Only humans are blasphemous—and this occurred only recently. If you are in the habit of blaming others (or God) for your problems, you will be expected to repent and make restitution for it.

What can compensate for being blasphemous? We are not angels. We cannot concentrate on such matters, but they are here. Your Spiritual Guides will be told. No need to sit and guess.

It will be the end before you can blink an eye—so be busy. Time is not long now. In the world's work today are many ways of the past: construction of dams, forts, and homes is similar, and you continue to figure out mathematical problems, but you do not honor God now. Past generations had the love of God within them and devoted their time and efforts to God, but not you all. We will discuss this now.

If the work of a day is not of God, it will never last. It will be redone before the next day is over. You will see this happen. You will also see God does not expect perfection, but man does. You expect everyone to see as you do, but you are wrong. All see in different ways. All learn in different ways. All work in different ways. No two people work alike—ever!

To expect people to compete for wages is not the best way to get a job done. The best way is to let people decide which work suits them best, and then let them do that work. All work will then get done.

You do not trust God, so how can you trust man? That is definitely *your* problem—not ours. We are here to help you, but we cannot be everything. If the help we give is not enough, you need to ask your Guides for help. Help is always available from others in the upper planes who guide all out of this Earth plane. You can find others on Earth who may be able to help, too, because this is not a project without direction. However, you are without direction and none from other worlds within this sphere are here to help you leave.

In the beginning of this time *you* asked for time. You asked for divisions that could be counted and arranged into orderly patterns. Seasons are the result of this, as well as days, weeks, and months. You need never fear the weather will chill to such a degree that you cannot live, but you need to worry that you will be unable to advance to the next plane by the time Earth collides with another planet.

THE WORK BEGINS

You are not the only one to call attention to The World's needs, but You are the only one who can help *you*. We are here and will help you be on guard against false prophets, but the rest is up to you. Many will announce the end, but few have details. If the end was revealed to them, ask for details. You will now see that these *words written here* will be repeated and repeated by many who claim to know much, but you know as much as they do now. Read this material and know!

Why you need to follow is in-bred. You were all soldiers in the past. You all had many lives of fortune and fame. You all needed to come together now to help new souls without long experience in Earth's ways to avoid being killed before their time. The work of The World is not war, but war caused all of you to seek peace. No one who has not warred can know peace. If the world is not at peace, you will see it come to be.

The time has come to prepare for the end—when all is known. Once the end is here, it is too late to join classes of restitution. You must do that now. All the worries of your life concern making restitution for things you fear are not right, because you must do that. The time to begin making restitution is now—not later.

Once you prepare for the end, the end is no longer a frightening idea. You will be eager to get to the next plane, but do not be so eager that you shorten your life in any way on this plane. You disturb the schedule, so those above would most likely send you back. We are here to see people go forward and not be returned, so we do not want that to happen. Never seek to kill yourself or let your body think you wish to die, since that is another way to end life and would produce the same effect as suicide.

When you are ready to die (as you call it), we will help you cross over to the other side. You then wait for a short time until the vaporization of your body is complete. Once this is accomplished, you begin a lengthy examination of your work on Earth. This examination and degree of time spent on it is determined by High Guides presiding over your life. You will learn more and more about this as we go along.

In many ways you are not the only beings who question God, but you are the only ones who blame God. We seek to know why you believe you are not responsible for your own decisions and actions. This is a very strange idiosyncrasy of the human race—and we will not tolerate it. You must change it at once!

The idea that God would destroy you or condemn you to death for a past life is outrageous. You will not be allowed to teach such destructive ideas. If you do, the work will be given to others who know man's place on Earth.

In the past we were never able to enter the realm of earthly work, because it was not of the upper planes; but now that we are here and asked to help, we want to reassure you that nothing is so bad here that it cannot be mended. It is unlikely that *you* can do it.

We seek those who can build and construct dams, but they are not available. They are all into numbers. They can see things are not done well, but know not how to correct it, so they resort to numbers.

Computers are unable to do physical work, so why are they now placed above people? Computers are the advanced toys of a race of people who do not know what to do next. Computers have been here before. The only thing new is *you*. You never remember the end of one life, so how could you remember when computers were on Earth before?

If you need toys, you need help!

We will help you discreetly change in such a way that few will notice until it is over and you are strong enough to withstand their assaults and attempts to revamp you into their ways. However, we will never let you sway others. You are not here to do missionary work. That was why some came to Earth, but now is the time to get out.

You need all the time you have to do your own work. The others will be told, and if others are aware of God, they will prepare. If they do not realize now the depth of their pain and suffering on Earth, they will. You do not need to care either way about it. If you brought forth children upon the Earth, it is necessary to instruct them in the ways of God; but once they grow into adults, it is their life and they are responsible for it.

The work of today is to be ready when the days are long and drawn out, yet you cannot end your life. You may feel it is too long to wait, but you must. Life is to be lived until the very end.

If you waste time at the end, you will have committed a sin. You must not sit alone and idle.

You need to seek outside experiences if you are confined to your body. If you wish to travel without leaving your house, it is not difficult to do. Many today do it frequently. You will see it constantly now that we have mentioned it to you. People call it *out-of-body*, but it is not. You are confined to the body, but not confined to the same location. You have to return to your body, and there is no way to loosen that tie. Once you reach the end of your tether, you must return. The tether is not long, but it lets you explore in a safe environment—much like a pony or dog not permitted to run wild for its own safety.

If you cannot travel, we suggest you meditate. The subject taught here always comes back to meditation. Does it not? We will constantly refer to meditation, but it is your responsibility to master it. You should meditate as often as possible.

We see people often call *The Scribe* and ask for recommendations for meditation books. Why? Why do you need to read about it? You can do it easily! Just sit still and look at nothing. Breathe in and out and count the breaths. No message or answers will be received or given while you count. You merely listen to your breath.

The only way to breathe is through your lungs. Most of you do not breathe deep enough to be of real benefit to your lungs, so they rot. If you breathed fresh, clean air into the lungs daily, how could disease live? It would be eliminated. Is it too difficult to breathe correctly?

Now The World is not at all like you, but then you are not of The World. You are not of Earth, either. You live here and dwell on the surface of Earth, while others dwell within it. You live in the light while others live in the dark, but you all live on one planet. It is no problem. You live separately and do not enter into the lives of one another. You do not look alike. If you are not alone here, how will the others escape? We will answer that now. Earth is not being preserved, because you entered and destroyed it; but because others here had no part in this destruction, they are being preserved—because God does not destroy life.

God prepares you for growth. You are told to grow and multiply, but you do not have to begin to grow while on Earth. You are here to develop into the best possible human you can be, but that is not the same as being human. The rest of Earth has the same assignment. Once you can understand that God exists in every living thing and everything is alive, you will be better able to know God.

If you are unable to understand Earth, we will help you enter caves and develop a sense of the enormous capacity of God to build within a set framework. Earth is constantly changing and altering its structure, but Earth does not need you to completely alter it. You were sent here to develop *you*—not Earth. Earth has its own work.

You are surprised that Earth is a giant organism?

We are surprised you do not realize that fact already. We are here to help you understand the working of God, but it is amazing that all of you have lived here so many lives and still are ignorant about Earth. This is not good, but we will help to improve your concept of why you are here and what you must do now to escape the end.

If the end of The World is not at the same time as the end of Earth, you will see its destruction, but we prefer that it not happen. We see many want to witness the death of the planet, but that is unkind. Increasingly, you have acted in idiotic and inhumane ways toward one another, so how can we expect you to be able to comprehend the destructiveness of people who raped Earth.

If the end of Earth comes before the end of The World, you will be able to see first-hand the results of your idle ways. You began the destruction and now moan about it. How is this possible? Why are you shocked that Earth is shrinking? You have exploded bombs, drilled for oil, and depleted vast seas of gas and oil for use on the surface. You only now see that the seas are polluted and fish are dying. You cannot even give up smoking—let alone stop setting forest fires—a fascination of some that destroys Earth. We will not condone any open fires. It is the end of the universe if all oxygen is consumed by one planet.

When you cannot enjoy life, you cause others to fear. It is a common trait among humans. We have observed it, and we are not amused. We will harm no one, but we are here to chastise those who are not listening to instructions given.

THE WORK BEGINS

You who are the abhorrers of work will know the time is near when you see angels. Why wait until then? If you cannot see angels, you are unable to see. We send you messages daily. We send them by way of angels, too. Angels are not only on Earth, but also in The World you live in. This atmosphere is being cleaned continually by angels. You need only look deeply into your vision field to see their vapor. Look at the sea and see them rise above it. Look over the tops of trees and there they are.

We send the people of Earth many messages, but few listen to them. You all will listen soon! The end of this message is now, but the messages will be developed for you over a long period of time and condensed into legible words that can be easily understood by most people. If you need help, come to us and we can open your mind. You need not call your Guides, if all you need is to open your mind to our teachings. Teaching is our job, and we do it best.

When you seek knowledge, you seek God

You will be asked to read. If that is not possible, we will read for you. Put out work that must be read and it will be entered into your mind. It is no big deal! We can do it easily!

Your eye is a computer, but has limited scope. We have no eyes, but we see. If your eyes grow weary and there is not enough time to read, you will know the material anyway. No trick—just a miracle!

Whenever you receive a miracle, ask God to help you to fully appreciate it so you may receive more. If you share your miracles, you can gain much more. But if you keep it all to yourself, we see no problem with that.

The work of today is over.

Chapter Eight

This world is not the only one to suffer...
If Earth is destroyed

In your knowledge you are the only ones living, but Earth is home to many others. If you are the only ones to be killed at the end, why would heavenly hosts be called in to help? Never since the beginning of all that is has there been such a time as this! We want to be there to help, but if there is no one to help, we will not be needed. The work will be done.

You must help Earth. Your race caused the trouble, but you see it not. We want you to see and understand why The World caused trouble for itself, so you will adjust the air and water. If air and water could be extended, many people living now might be able to transcend this world and develop into the next; however, there is not enough air and water now to give them time to do this.

We seek scientists who can help! If they are readers of this material, we seek them now. If they are unaware, we beseech you to tell them to read this!

In the work of The World are many who are not of God. We know this, yet find it difficult to believe. If The World is such an un-Godly place, how has it continued until now? We suggest you brought the universe down upon all of us, because you do not care.

How can such a work of God exist? You are created by God, but not controlled. You have been allowed to destroy so you might learn about power. It is not unlike a child left unattended. Why do that? We know not, but if you doubt it, you will learn you are the only one who doubts it.

In the work of God are many agents of *the other*. We never speak of this, but there is another power. There are only two powers: positive and negative. The power of positive is yours, but negative power does exist and is not to be underestimated. We often see it, but we were unaware of its terrible effects until we came to this place. You will be unable to understand this, so we will explain it in easy phrases.

The end of The World is not the end of the work of God, but it will be the end of negative influence. We see that only this world has had to deal with it. This atmosphere is very conducive to the work of evil. You do not dwell in evil—but in God. However, some are evil, and this life is not the work of God—rather the work of *the other*. You are not the only ones to work on the air and create goods. If The World is not the only society to live on Earth, then who else resides here?

We are unable to outline the entire course for you at one time, but you can learn the elements. Some revere earth, wind, fire, and the darkness of night as elements, but water is the only element. You exist in and are made of water. You are also made of certain elements that constitute air. They are the elements needed to keep you alive. If any elements are inadequate, the soul may not enter that body.

The soul is unable to enter a body if it cannot endure. The only people who live beyond the childhood stage are those who wish to live here a long time. Some souls come to Earth for only a short time in order to develop briefly and then return to the upper planes. They may be angelic beings or not. This time on Earth is seen only as a class—not an entire course of study.

Why do you wail and weep as though this personality is dead? The soul never dies! The soul is eternal. If it chooses to stay only a short time on Earth, you are not the only one to miss it, but it has other work to do.

If you think you are in charge, you are not. We are not in charge of Earth, either, but we have a sense of who is. You will not be able to please God, if you do not know who is in charge.

In the world of You there are several entities like *you*, but in flesh you are the only one on Earth. You are not here to become greater than God. You are here to be like God, but not a god. All who act like a god are unwelcome. We do not care if they are destroyed. Does that shock you? It is true! All who are not of God are against God and will bit-by-bit be left to die.

If *the other* is not to blame, then who is? You are! You are the only ones here who have the power to destroy Earth. No one else is that highly evolved, but you were not given this classroom to destroy! You were given an opportunity to develop Earth and continue to grow.

Never since the beginning has anything God created ever been as destructive as you people! If your own life is not a showcase of what you can do, what do you think you are doing now? You are that which you are.

You cannot take credit for the work of another at the end, although many of you do that every day of your life now. Some are misguided into believing that if you are perfect, you will go to heaven, but that is not a true concept. Although grounded in fact, the concept got twisted. You are to strive to be as good as you can be—but not perfect.

At the end you will be passed up to the next plane, but it is not heaven. You will be asked to pass several tests at the time of the crossing over from this plane to the next, and you must pass each if you are to be permitted to make the move. We offer only the following guidelines:

1. Work hard and do all you can each day. If the day ends and your work is done—good. If the day ends and your work is not complete—let it go. The work of one day cannot be completed the next day.

2. Social order is to be established and maintained. You are to be orderly—not seeking gain from others who have just enough. You have enough to live on, and they cannot spare much. If you steal from others, you create disharmony and imbalance. It is, therefore, a cardinal sin to steal.

3. If you are unable to raise your children, you must let them go. You must not force them to do your work or create a livelihood for you. The only ones who are to help you are adults. No children will be permitted to work for the adult population. If they do, their work will be destroyed.

4. You are never to take God for granted!

5. You are not here to be the only one on Earth, rather one of many serving the means and ends of God. If this is not your purpose, you have wasted your time here.

6. The many religions of Earth are not of God but of man. If none suit you, you will still be held accountable for worshiping God. The only people permitted to go beyond this plane are those who worship God. To worship is not the same as to follow a religion, but religionists usually discover that is within its center. Even if disenchanted, you are still responsible for permitting others to worship in peace.

7. You are not the only ones here on Earth to develop, but we are the only ones here to teach you. If you cannot heed what we teach, you will be asked to return to Earth.

In the end, all is the same ~
You will be!

You are not here to be the only victim or survivor of the holocaust, nor the only one on the way up. The end of The World is not now, but the work will become very difficult for those left here. It is always more difficult when the work was previously done by many hands and suddenly there are fewer to do it. If your work is incomplete when Earth is destroyed, you will have no time to do it. But if the work is done, you will go forward to the next plane.

We will not be there. We are not to help you cross over. That is the work of angels. Your work on Earth may well be of the angelic realm, but you are here to work as humans. If the work is not done, you will not be passed to the plane you came from—so *all of you* have much to be concerned about now.

In the work of your plane are many higher beings. These beings are here to develop a certain phase of their entire soul and are not to be destroyed. The only ones to be destroyed will be those who have never honored God. To honor God is why you are here—not to honor yourself or man. Those who preach you must love yourself first are preaching the end of man. In the love of self is nothing. You must be of God or you will be nothing.

We will now help you understand why self exists. Self is the part of You that exists on Earth. It is the only part here in flesh. You exist in many forms, but only this flesh is deadly. You may not destroy your flesh, but it dies. You can live and go to the next plane, but the body does not leave Earth. Your body is not of the heavens—it is of Earth and belongs here. We will go into it much deeper at a later time.

If the work of God is not self, then why are you here in flesh? We are not here to explain all that is to those who have had an eternity to find out, but we will tell you enough to refresh your memory.

The only work here of God is *you*, and if *you* are not *you*, you will be unable to cross over to the next plane. The work of *you* here is not the same as self. Self is and always will be the world's way of defining its work. You will be expected to accomplish much as an entity on Earth, yet not held accountable if that work is destroyed. You will be told to take the course over—which means you will be demoted to a lower plane to do this work again—which is not a good thing.

Whatever you do, do it well. If you cannot do your job correctly, get a job that suits you—but get a job! The work of self is the definition of how you choose to be while on Earth. If you are not the only one to choose it, and it is not big enough for all of you, some will have to reelect another job in order to successfully complete their stay on Earth. You will not be expected to complete the job of Earth, but you will be expected to complete your share of it. The work of Earth is not the same as the work of The World.

It is difficult to explain that Earth is not inanimate—but alive. This is a different way of seeing what you always accepted as being dead, but is alive—and that is the truth. Earth is a giant. It sleeps and dozes now, but at times comes to life and fully exerts its might. You have never seen it, but Earth can and does destroy all life. We have only to look over the history of Earth to see how many civilizations have been here and disappeared to know yours is not the only one to be destroyed, but yours is the only one to destroy Earth.

Whatever you do, you must never be guilty of destroying your host. You are an organism that thrives on Earth, but you are not the main entity. You are only aware of its power at times when the crust is mightily disturbed by inner turbulence, but it is far greater than you can imagine. What you need to do is help when called. If you help, we see no problem. If you do not help, you will never be permitted to take on new responsibilities and will be destroyed.

God has no further need for those who cannot obey. Obedience is a bad word in certain areas of the world today, and we are surprised by that. You will know if you are one of the few who recognize it.

We see children and adults run freely without any law and order. We wonder why this is, but you know. You are the only ones to enforce the law. If society does not believe in a law, it is eliminated; but today many laws exist in large areas that are of no use and are ignored. Is this the way of civilized people? Should not the laws be re-formed and made into a living body of work that controls and disciplines without ruining the souls of those who have been unable to develop into law-abiding citizens?

The only ones who can change laws are those who keep them, but you elect people who are lawbreakers. Does this really matter? We think so. If your lawmakers are also lawbreakers, no one else can be expected to obey the laws. If no one obeys your laws, you are all lawless. To be lawless is a state of anarchy, and anarchy is not for the people but against them. When a lawmaker continues to do evil, the law is besmirched;

THE WORK BEGINS

but if that lawmaker is made to suffer for the evil, the law is upheld. You must uphold the law starting at the top and the bottom will not be so unruly.

All who live are not of Earth, but many are. You may or may not be of Earth, but you live on Earth now. For this reason, you must be able to transcend it at the end or risk being destroyed. The World you live in is not attuned to this end.

Most of you fear only the end of your work on Earth. No one thinks of the end of Earth without fear, but then many of you never think about the end of *you*. We are! We want *you* to transcend evil and live.

Whatever you do, do your work. Do not worry over the work of others. If you do your work and have time left over to help others, you may assist, but you may never set out to do another person's work for them. It is against the rules of God to do the work of another. Your life is your work. The other people on Earth have their work to do, and if they do not do it, you are not held responsible for it. But if you did not do your work, because you were doing someone else's work, you are held responsible for not being ready. You will understand as time goes on that it is not your worry alone—but everyone's that all are passed to the other side and the next plane. If you do not cooperate, you will be in danger of being held back.

∼

If this session is not understood, you are not ready to continue to the next lesson. We recommend you sit and meditate and develop a plan for how you must do your work now. If your Guides pass the plan, it will be approved for you to do. If your new plan is not approved by your Guides, we will check it out. The only time High Guides are involved is if a plan might adversely affect the rest of your race. The High Guides are not here to help. They are judges of this world—and not pleased now. That is why we are here.

If the work of the soul is to be ready to join God, you can always find plenty of work. If you believe this life is it, you will be sadly disappointed at the end.

We offer you this proof of God ~ YOU!

If You disappear, is it because *you* did not exist or because you were never here? We see you are often unable to understand even small problems such as this one, so how could you begin to understand God? You cannot, so let it go and get busy at the work you came to do.

Chapter Nine

Many are now announcing the end of time, but it is not the end! It may be the end of Earth, perhaps, or the end of your world, but it is not THE END. You are only one small fraction of the total work of God.

You do not care for the outer work of many people and know nothing of their inner work—nor should you. It is not the business of humans to know the work of others. It is *your* work you must concentrate upon, and if you do not, you have to repeat your lesson. We do not want you to repeat.

If the work of this world is incomplete, and it will be if you do not work hard every day, you will be unable to go further and will be expected to continue on your current assignment. How can you go further if there is no Earth? You will learn, if you are stupid enough to wait for that to happen. We suggest you do not wait.

You ask, "Why would God inflict pain?" We are not here to identify pain or why God has no interest in stopping your reality of it. We are here to identify how you can enjoy the peace of God and continue to grow into the Light. We do not care for your concepts of pain, sorrow, anger, and fleshly desires, but it is as you designed it this time. God did not intrude into your desire to be totally self-centered, either. You chose to do it this way.

All want to be free of pain and sorrow now. No one wants it anymore, but how do you free yourself of it? You *all* decide to be free of it! Once the decision to be free of pain and sorrow is reached—and it will be, you may decide to never again let it enter your hearts or minds, but we think that would be an over-reaction.

Let the heart of man become a place of peace and understanding—and let the mind be calm. Once the aims of both are achieved, you can decide in what direction to grow. Only then can you be *you*.

Welcome change!

Never let change happen without trying to improve the lot of man. If you do not change, you die. If you die trying to change, you may have made it to the next plane; but if you die without trying to change, you will stay here. We suggest strongly that you try to end this Earth's domination over your soul and begin to enter into the work of God while still on Earth, instead of waiting until the next plane is achieved.

If you cannot do much work of this world, you may not be able to proceed to the next plane; but if the work of Earth is easy for you to do, you may be on the next plane while here. This is a startling conclusion—is it not?

THE WORK BEGINS

We now concur with the higher planes in their desire to raise you all above this plane and do it quickly, so we are not holding you back from experimenting with channeling and other methods of contacting God within you at this time. We are, in fact, encouraging you to try. Once you master the method you prefer, we can teach you direct. You will not need a teacher then, but you should not become vain. If you become vain and decide you know all there is to know, you will be taught a lesson—a lesson we will not reveal now, but one which you will remember.

If the work of God is not the work of your soul, you will not be ready for advancement. If the end of Earth arrives while you are still here, your soul will be thirsty—not you. Your soul is trying to complicate your life so you seek peace now. If you seek peace, you seek God.

We are here for all who want our help, but we never intrude into the life of any human. No one ever intrudes into your life! Only you have the power to let someone else persuade you to change your life. If you let others persuade you—and you do, you must realize it is not the last time or the first time for you to make that choice. You will make many thousands of choices that alter you while on Earth—and each choice is your own to make, but you may not realize it then.

When your life is complicated by the demands of others, you often believe you must consider their needs above your own, but that is not true. You must first consider your own needs—then the needs of anyone you brought into this world—only then do you consider the needs of others.

We watch women seek men to improve their financial standing in the world and see them sorry once they have found it. We are not interested in your financial standing. We are not interested in your intellectual pursuits. We are only interested in you—the real *you*.

If you do nothing to enhance what you brought to this life, you are a failure. If you change all you were given then, you are a failure because you do not appreciate the real reason you came to Earth. If you change all you came to Earth to change and still need to be busy, we will help you detect your reason for being.

Your everlasting reason for being is not to be shared. It is to be reached after long and arduous climbing over the obstacles placed in your way by The Almighty. You may not realize it at the time, but the climb is what makes you strong. You feel yourself grow and reach within for strength that enables you to understand why you are *you*. You will never be able to explain it, *but you will know!*

If the work of your heart is not open to the work of others, you will never be able to share in their delight or *dis-ease*, nor will you be able to learn from them. Would you prefer to be free of all people? If you answer, "Yes," you will be unable to understand why you are here on Earth. You must understand people before you can rise higher than humanity. If you do not understand, you will not be elevated. We see you can understand that.

THE WORK BEGINS

*Now let us sit and ponder this:
What is the real reason you are not happy?*

We know all about the silly, inconsequential matters which surround you daily and are not easy to endure, but we are referring to the essential You—not the human being sitting and reading this book. What does it take to make *you* happy? Why are you not always happy? What if you could be happy, would you be happy?

We can see you do not know what happiness is, thus unable to know if you can be happy. Happiness is the art of living! It is the means of being *you* and all it means to be You. If you are not happy, you are not *you*.

When The World is finished with its games, but you are not ready to be elevated to the higher planes, what do you plan to do? We see that you think this is unimportant. What is more important to you than ascending at the end of this life?

We are not here to do penance, but you are. If you are not ready for the next plane, you will remain behind. If you cannot conduct your life on Earth, how can you deserve a better one? This is the only life for some of you. You will not be given another in order to deceive The World.

You are not the only beings on Earth, but you do not exist in any other world. You are present on Earth to do certain things, but if you deny the work of God—and that worldly events are your creation, you will be unable to inherit the Earth or advance to the next plane. Only those who have failed, but tried, can return to Earth at some point. If you never tried to change events, or tried to be different from others, or helped others be safe or happy, you will not be allowed to continue living on Earth.

~

What happens to a soul not permitted to advance or return to Earth?

We are not permitted at this time to discuss the repercussions of such a wasted life, but in the future it may be allowed. It is better to let such matters rest and develop a strategy to insure you are not in such a position to learn what happens.

What if Earth ends and you are still here? We see you listen to many who predict Earth will be gone soon, but you do not actually believe it. Why ask? If your life on Earth is mostly your own doing, why do you believe God would want it? You know it is no easy place to be, but you chose to be here. That is the answer to all your questions!

We are unable to help anyone who is not ready. We cannot expect those who are ready to wait for others to grow and develop, but we can ask you to help those who may need to be encouraged to hurry. If you enable another soul to leave Earth, you are always blessed.

We encourage your help by giving you greater gifts of The Holy Spirit. You will seek out these gifts on your own, but never consistently present them until such time as they are *given* to you. You know if you are *psychic* or not, but you may not teach it to others. It is not yours to give. It is a feeling within that cannot be taught. If you desire to become *psychic* or spiritual, we will help—but only if you care enough to meditate daily. If you cannot meditate, you cannot advance into the spiritual realm.

You can meditate,
It is your choice!

If you are unable to realize the moment, how can you live now? We suggest you concentrate on NOW and forget the past, and let go of the future. If you do not care for the ways of the past—change them. However, if the past taught you much, you should continue to keep it as it was.

The last few decades on Earth have been times of retrieval. You all seek what was set aside and/or forgotten by previous generations, which is a smart way to advance. You must enjoy the knowledge that there is a rhythm and rhyme to all that exists and you are not the only being. If you cannot enjoy such knowledge, you will never appreciate the depth of work man has done on Earth—and your passage will be a failure.

You must enjoy life!

If the work of this world is not to your satisfaction—and it is not for many of you, then you must decide how you can change your area. If you let your life go and do nothing, you will enhance the lives others are building around you, but if you change your life and the area around you, others may decide to change and accept your ways, too. You can be a winner regardless of whether or not they accept your ways; however, you cannot win if you do not accept the ways of Earth and act upon them now.

You have been allowed to enter Earth in order to prepare for advanced work. If you do not do your work now, you will obviously be unable to advance. It is no difficult matter to understand. We see you do not believe life is so simple, but it is.

If you came to Earth in order to achieve a lot of difficult work, you may have selected an environment of challenge or a body of little ability to carry out all you desire, so you might develop more than you would under ordinary circumstances.

The real reason for developing to another plane is to increase your ability to love. If you cannot love while on Earth, how may you grow? We suggest you learn to adopt another person and help that person grow. The problem is there, and if you do well, you will advance. If you do not deserve to advance, you will be unable to give of yourself or receive the love of others.

The time to change is while you are on Earth, because you cannot repeat this lesson. It is not the kind of assignment that advances you to another plane, but it does cost you a lifetime—so get on with it.

We are aware of large numbers of humans who cannot develop beyond the adolescent stage due to increased numbers of people on Earth. If all were adults, the population would increase at such a high rate none could live; however, are the ones populating Earth now the ones who should be here?

We seek only the brave, strong, and daring, but you like the weak and ineffective to govern. Why? We believe from observing you all that it is because you fear the superiority of others. You have not learned to be humble. You believe you alone are the best. You think others are not as keen or smart as you are and not enthusiastic about other's ideas.

We seek out the elders, but you revile them. That is the lesson of youth—the lesson of age is wisdom. If you are not wise, you are foolish. The fact is: the people of Earth are not young. You have all been on Earth many times. You need to remember your youth and change now—to accept the wisdom of elders. If you do not remember the elders now, you will.

In times to come you will not be asked for your ideas. You will be asked about what you can do to help others gain access to High Guides and others from the upper planes. If you do not have access to them, how can you help others? We suggest you listen until the end of this session—then develop many ideas that make sense to you now. If your ideas are not on track, we will sort them out and destroy any that would harm you in any way.

Begin sitting still and letting the words run together. Relax deep into your seat and let your mind wander. Once the mind has cleared out the residual of outer world needs, you can begin reading again.

Welcome to the work of God!

If you need time to adjust to the work of God, you will be given enough time. But if you refuse to work, your life will end short of the time allotted to you to be on Earth. Why should this plane be taken up with souls who are not yet ready to ascend?

What you must do is send up a list of work you plan to do to increase your worth. If the list is long, you may not be allowed to leave Earth until it is completed; therefore, list only the most important ideas you have for improving *you* now. Once the list is complete, begin to work. It will take the rest of your life to do it well, but it will be done before you leave. This list is not the only list you will be asked to prepare, but it is the most important one. For that reason, we will add a few details here:

1. List all the ways you need to be free of outside distractions in order to achieve internal peace and calm. If your life is too complex, you must think of it as being simple—then how to make it stay that way.

2. You are not allowed to deny others access to the work of your spirit, but you do not have to access others' work. You need not read or study others' work or do it like they did it—and you must not run down the work of others, either.

3. If your list is to be read and studied, you must word it so others cannot comprehend its meaning to *you*. The work of your spiritual self is not to be discussed with others. *You* are the only one on your pilgrimage. You will not worry

about others accompanying you—ever. They have their own Guides and lists to follow.

4. We are unable to identify your Guides, but you can do it whenever you desire help. However, you are the only one who does your work. No Guide can do it for you! Only you have the power to work on *you*. All others are here merely to aid you at this time—and will not be with you forever.

5. List only the things *you* need—not what you learned elsewhere. If you do not need something you now believe is absolutely necessary for your further development, you will be able to ignore it. Do not waste time on things you know how to do and currently use to develop your inner sources.

6. If you do not meditate, you will waste this lifetime on Earth.

7. If you meditate, but seldom ask for help then, you will take much longer to accomplish things. Please ask for help. Many are waiting to hear from you now.

8. Your anger is not the same as God's anger, but it can be used to control those around you who try to abscond with your work. If you do a work of worth and others try to take credit for it, you *may* be exempted from stress caused by anger. Normally, stress is the result of anger and must be avoided for that reason. No other stress is quite as bad as anger not vented correctly.

9. Humility is considered the worst sin in your world today, but is the only virtue you must seek now. You will begin by not taking credit for God entering your life or work. All who ask are to be told you are entering into a new *you* and can now do what you desire.

10. We are not going to list what you need, but you will be able to do it if you sit and discuss within you what makes you happy. If you feel sad, let it float and see where it takes you. It may end up making your list a bit shorter.

We suggest your list contain no more than three items. If it is much longer, it is too hard to achieve. You must be able to work on it at all times. Once an item is learned, it is dropped. Your life is long enough to take care of all that needs to be done, but if you have extra time, we will let you select another area to advance in while you are here on Earth.

The only list you have now is the one you started when you set out to read this book, but soon your mind will shatter the past. You will remember only the one you are now. The list you then create is the one you will work on until you die.

Your death, of course, is no big deal to us, but to humans it is the end of flesh. Make sure it is! We want you to advance to the next plane and not return to Earth. This is our only assignment, and we do not want to fail. We are judged by your acceptance and others of our work. If we fail to enlist you into the realm of God this time, we will be unable to teach again—and for a teacher, there is no greater punishment.

If the work of this session is difficult, you will notice an increase in your energy level. Always exert yourself! If you do not, you will feel energy oozing from you. Remember, energy grows in those who exert themselves. Energy begets energy. You can feel it.

THE WORK BEGINS

As the last item for today's class, let us all begin to understand why The World is not Earth and Earth is not the way God created it. We want all of you to be able to instruct others in the simple economics of keeping Earth free of all contaminants and evil until the last possible moment.

Evil is not a free and inexpensive way to live—as so many humans believe. It is the most costly of all decisions you will ever make. It will end your line. It will cost you your life. It will not advance your soul or your spirit to the next plane. It is the worst way to live.

Think before you do evil to anyone!

The only way to be free of evil is to be free. If you are tied up in knots—unable to enjoy life, you are unable to let others enjoy life, too. Jealousy and hatred grow, if you are unhappy. You must be able to enjoy *you*. If you cannot, your life on Earth is short and ugly, rather than long and sweet. We will not help anyone who hurts others, because that is a strong, sure way to be left on Earth until its destruction.

Mockery of all that is God is the surest way anyone can devise to be left until the end, so let it go and ignore the calls of others to abandon what you know to be true. If you are unable to withstand the sort of ignorance that often abounds within a small community, you would not be expected to set out for a distant city, but would have to work harder to ignore the ignorance where you are. It may be the best way to grow up.

If the work you do now is not helping you develop into the kind of person you wish to be, you will need to change it. It is no different than if you are raised in a family that encourages evil. You must change any area that interferes with being *you*, but do not hurt others as you make such changes.

It takes time to extract yourself from a pit of vipers, but it can be done. You will be given extra credit for not killing anyone who deserves to be slain, but if you kill someone with intent, you will be taken and expect to return to Earth to fulfill that life. It is not a good way to advance your soul. It is penance.

If your life is not as difficult as it was in your youth, you may not relax now. You still have work to do. You cannot sit and stare at the wall or a television when you have to meditate and work out details of your life so there will be little to sort through when you cross over. If your life has any areas still not right, you can correct them now and you should. Do not sit still or death of this life will come too quickly.

When you are ready to go to the next plane, angels will be there. If you are to be returned, no angels appear, but your Guides will be there to help you select the best way to repay for a lost life. If angels appear to you now, you may rest assured they are here to help you gain access into the upper realms and will help you cross over at the end. We will not go into it further later, but know this is true.

THE WORK BEGINS

Welcome the work of God
And know it is good!

We will be there if you need instruction—otherwise call upon your Spiritual Guides for anything you need. You may be surprised at how full of happiness and gayety you and all around your life can be now. Life is not meant to be a time of pain and sorrow. That is your idea of life—not ours or anyone above you—certainly not God's way.

Chapter Ten

The work of this session will be concerned with the development of *you* as a personality. You are not *you* until you reach maturity—and maturity is not given to people. It must be attained and worked upon once it is reached in order to develop into the entire being you are meant to be. If you do not advance while on Earth, you will not be allowed to advance higher, so we are here to help you advance now in whatever area you may seriously lag behind the majority of other people.

In spiritual work the only means of control is the way you feel. In physical work, you feel and look, and if the feel of something is not quite right, you look and see what it is. In spiritual work there is no need to look—you just know!

For all who are unable to advance,
We will start at the beginning.
For all who are ready to go,
This will be a review.

First, let no one else be you or impersonate *you* in any way. You are the only one to be here on Earth in your guise. No one else is exactly like you—not even an identical twin! Begin immediately to differentiate yourself from all others. That does not mean you are to act odd or wear strange clothes and behave like an idiot. It means you are to identify what sets you apart from all others and develop such traits.

If you are talented in the area of work, you will be expected to excel in the workplace. If your ability lies elsewhere, you are not to be held back because you did not excel in the workplace. You must work, of course, but it is not necessary to be a *star*, as you say. Work to the best of your abilities and do all you can to improve the job assigned to you. You will not be expected to create new jobs for others unless that is your special talent.

Once you discover the latent ability which is *you*, your life is more meaningful and distinct. You feel like *you* and look like you, but your work is only beginning then. You must proceed to develop that ability and organize your time so it can all be done. If you stop work in order to develop a special realization of yourself, you are in danger of being left behind.

We do not condone the abandonment of a career or cessation of work, but you may change occupations if the original one is not worthy of you. This is rarely ever the case, but it happens. You need only look to *The Scribe* to know that.

If your life is not good for you—and it may not be, you must change it to become the way you are now. If your life is not fulfilling all your needs, you must improve areas lacking substance. We will help anyone who feels you deserve more than you have, but you must work, too.

THE WORK BEGINS

No one ever believes they are paid what they deserve; and fortunately for many, that is true. Welcome the interest you earn from doing a job on Earth that is not well paid. When the time is here to account for this life, it is not judged by the amount of money earned, but how well you did the work.

If your social patterns run counter to those of the area in which you live, you may seek another area. If the social pattern you decide to adopt is different from the area you move to, you will have many more problems than you can handle in one lifetime. Be careful to always analyze every change *before* you make it—not afterwards.

If you take care, your reward will be many spiritual walls able to grow within you. In the walls of *you* are many vibrations. These vibrations are organized into several different strata. The strata are not social orders, but can be compared to them. We prefer to organize your life by strata rather than at the *vibrational* level since time is short. To explain how it works, we will take you back to the beginning.

In the beginning of human development there is a wave of energy that surfaces and ignites the genes so you can become a particular person with specific traits. This genetic surgery occurs at the time you are conceived, even though you are not *you* at that moment. You become a tiny microorganism, and then a big burst of energy boosts the building of cells and eliminates any that cannot make the long journey to birth. This is a spontaneous effort to rid the body of anything not ready to be developed into a viable human. If you interfere with this process, you are playing God.

God does not confer honors on anyone who desecrates the creative work or contemplates murdering the individual. You are not to abort a baby once it begins to grow beyond the stage of maturity, i.e., it is developed into a personality and can be sensed by the mother as stirring within her. Often the fetus emotionally affects the woman before it begins to breathe—even though it is not living as a human then. Once you feel the heart beating and the coolness at center occurs, you are in charge of another human being and must respect that honor. You will not have to return if you are guilty of such a death and have repented, but it will hurt your advancement. If you have read this material and then decided to terminate a pregnancy, you will be returned and expected to live out another life to compensate for it.

While you live on Earth, it is not necessary for you to tell others how to live. They have their own Spiritual Guides—God created them. If God is not concerned about them, you can have no concern, either. What some people do is not what you must do, but you must let them do their work in their own way. This is a problem for some parents because of their need to control bad behavior in the early years of a child—and as a result, cannot stop trying to control others. You must end such conceits immediately. If you do not, your life is in danger of being pushed back, and you will be expected to repeat this life.

THE WORK BEGINS

Whatever you do, you must do it well. If your life is not as you dreamed it would be, you can always change the dream—or *you* can change. It is always easier to change the dream, but it may not be as interesting. The choice is always yours.

God does not interfere with your dreams, but you often hear the voice of God within them. We are not dreams or agents who operate within your dreams, but your Spiritual Guides often operate within your dreams. For that reason alone, you should respect all dreams and analyze them. If you cannot do this, there are those who can help you. You must work to discover their hidden meanings, because the work is part of your spiritual development—and at the same time it enhances this life.

When you can do something well, you cannot share your secret, because you do not know why you can do it better than others. If you do know, you must teach it, because that is why you were given the gift. So many are here to teach now that we cannot comprehend all you may need, but we are ready to help you at any time. Because of the need for speed, begin to imagine yourself teaching others! Once you are teaching, you will be blessed with all you need to know. Until then, you must read and study, since a teacher must be able to discuss all materials related to the subject, but need not be an expert on all subjects. It is better to be short of material than to be long of wind.

When you cannot help others, it is not held against you. But if you can help and do not, you will be placed on a list of those who need to learn a lesson. We need you to avoid being placed on such lists, instead be ready to progress along the path you decided to develop prior to entering the Earth plane. If you do not add work to your assignment, you can easily transfer to the next plane; but if you added work, it may be another lifetime before you can arrive at the crossover point.

If The World you live in is not good for you, or you do not like being in it, you may ask for another life, but you still have to do whatever you can to fulfill this one. If your reasons are sound, and you are not to be punished for not living out this life, you will be granted another chance. However, if you decide to change your life on your own and do not control your ego, you will be granted no additional time to seek another way to live and will be expected to complete this life as you ordered it.

You do order your life!

Whatever you are doing now, it is because you choose to do it!! We cannot emphasize that enough. You are not the only person or the only soul to be elevated, but your soul's work is only what counts to You.

You will be expected to harm no other soul. You must not count on earning points by helping others advance. The points you earn in this life are not meant to help you advance from Earth, but help you establish the direction of your entry into the Light, once you are beyond this plane. If you do not do what is needed to transfer to the next plane, all such points accumulate until you cross over.

What another person does is not your worry. In fact, worry is not acceptable in your spiritual life, since it does not reflect trust in God. You are to adopt a worry-free attitude if you do not have it already. Your *worries* are not the same as worry. Worry as we see it is not at all without guilt, but *worries* about how to proceed with this life are necessary if you are to achieve the highest level of performance. You do not have to worry about such *worries*. This is not meant to be facetious, but it is always better to laugh then cry.

If your life is so deep in worry you cannot move, you are depressed and must release such tension immediately. We will help you do that. You need only ask God for a better mood. It truly is that simple!

If your life is not steeped in worry, and you fear nothing, you can move forward at a much faster pace than previously. We are here to shorten the time it takes to manifest all you desire, but you must be able to energize the atmosphere. If your atmosphere is not clear of debris, it can short circuit the work you plan to do, so clear the air before you start a new project.

To clear the atmosphere around you, simply ask your Spiritual Guides for advice on how to best navigate around obstacles so it can happen. You can differentiate between snags and obstacles, but may not be aware of it now. We will call attention to your work. If you notice it running into snags constantly, it is because your Guides are trying to attract your attention to what is wrong. You must choose a different route if the one you are on is blocked, or you cannot proceed with haste. The best time to change your route is before you invest a lot of energy into pursuing it. If that has happened, sit still and regain as much energy as possible, then proceed down a different path. If the path you choose is not good for you, seek the reason. Analyze the difference between success and failure and you will find it is simply because you did not analyze the work enough.

We are not here to regroup and rethink the way you and your societies are now, but it is necessary for you to do so. Without delay you must rethink why you do all you do to each other. The only reason for being on Earth is to learn how to deal with negativity, but some of you have embroidered this concept with many layers of worthless entanglements that have snared many good souls. Those of you who are able to understand must work to reduce the level of conflict in this world so you may be able to change into the best possible being you can be.

If you do not work at it, do you think those who are satisfied with the way things are will change it? Never! The reason you are not changing the world now is because you are satisfied. If you are dissatisfied with anything, you change everything. If you are only upset by minor difficulties, you will only tinker with major work. As you can see, you are in charge of this world—and you like it as it is or you would change it.

You mourn the sudden death of someone you know, because you cannot hold that person within your life—which is not the purpose of being on Earth. You are here to work on *you*, but often grow close to another human—which is fine, provided you do not merge. You are to remain independent all this life so you do not have to return. If you merge with another, your life is unable to achieve all you requested to do at this time, so you will be returned. Eliminate this possibility by sharing your life with others, but not being too attached to another.

If the death of another does not affect you in any way, you lost touch with humanity. You must realize you are here only for a very short time, but in this life with a large number of other souls who are here for the same reason as you—to develop spiritually while working with negative forces in a physical environment.

You are a positive energy field, and Earth is filled with negativity—which does not mean it is evil. You are not evil and you are of God. Why would God create someone or something greater than you? Obviously, it is you who creates such monsters—not God. We will touch upon evil later, but for now, let us concentrate on why you need it.

If the work you came here to do is not done by the end of this life, you may resort to telling stories about why you could not get it done on time. These stories are not respected by the higher planes, but get some play time here on Earth. These fables are not valuable, except to those who believe in them; nevertheless, many others are still influenced by them.

One such story is that God created angels and there was one angel who was so powerful it concentrated energy until such a time as it could overthrow the power of God. Such a story is blasphemy and does not bear repeating, but it is heard and wondered about even now. We will not let anyone reading this material continue to present to others foolish ideas as having validity.

God is God!
No angel is above God

You are not lower than the angels, but angels are not human. You will come across people, however, who are angels living on Earth in order to explore the means by which humans are tempted. If you come across one, you will be unaware of any difference, but an angel is different from *you*. We will identify one angel so you may know, but you will not become an angelic being. You are here to join the higher planes and work toward that end, but you are not an angelic being while on Earth.

Only angels are angels! Not one of the many, many people who claim to know angels can call angels to them. The work of calling angels is not for humans. It is the work of your Spiritual Guides. You must not call angels or ask angels to do your work—or you will be returned to Earth to learn humility.

If this message is not received, many will be harmed, but you are to know this *before* you call and not be upset if you called angels in the past. Only you know if you asked angels to do your work, but you are forgiven if it was done out of ignorance. You will not be forgiven if you know better, yet ask for an angel to help you do what you decide you want to do. That blasphemy can result in a far worse fate than having to relive this life. It can result in a total annihilation of your soul's existence. Angels are of God!! You must never forget that—ever!

Many of you seek God now because you are unhappy. If the work of the world satisfies you, most likely you would not be seeking God now. We are not upset that some are dissatisfied but still do not seek God—that is why we are here.

In the book that began this course of study (*We Are Here*), you were told why we are here, but we often repeat very important material in the event you may not have read the first volume. If this is repeat material to you, know it is not done without much thought. You will recognize you heard it once, but may not have acted upon it. The second time you learn of a matter, you are held accountable for not heeding it. The third time you ignore it, you refute the integrity of the material and are no longer given advice.

You must decide if you are to live by yourself or enjoy the peace and happiness that comes from working as a team with your Spiritual Guides, and all they enlist to help you.

What else does Earth need? You are the only one here to know why you do not help Earth recover from past ravages, but we also know why you do not help. You fear it will make you look ridiculous. You are ridiculous if you do not save your area. You are the only one who cares about your area, so if you do not act, who will?

The next reason for this session is that you cannot achieve the most from life if you do not realize why you are here. The reason is buried in your psyche and will be revealed when you are ready. If you never get to that point, you will lose. We want all of you to prepare for the time when *you* are You. You can begin by working on why you chose to enter the Earth plane this time.

If you are here on Earth to work out a past difference, you can do that before you leave the cocoon of your family; but if the reason you are here is to enjoy the freedom of Earth and its many different worlds, you will be unable to start your own life's work until all of Earth's work is done. You must do your daily work daily, so you can move to the highest stratum of this plane and begin your life's work.

This is the only time you are on your way to the end. You must not let it go without watching to see why you are not working to end your journey on Earth. If you end your travel to Earth, you will not be missed here; but if you miss Earth, you can be delivered here in another time and place or as an agent of God. We see many think you will return as angels, but that is not a foregone conclusion you can arrive at while on Earth. You are to be the only one of your soul to live here, but the soul has many other living aspects. You are only one of many, many aspects of your soul, but the only one on Earth at this time.

We can now write as a team, but you cannot. You must not work as a team, because it is your life you are responsible for when the time comes to count points. If you work as a team, your numbers are confused and your points diminish.

THE WORK BEGINS

You are to remain single only until you are ready to marry and begin a family. If you remain single in order to delay raising a family, and your life on Earth is not over until your responsibility to children has been met, this delays your passing over to the next plane, thus we do not advise you to marry late. When you marry late and decide to raise children, you may not be able to do so.

Many souls become despondent, because while here on Earth you know not what to do to pass the time between birth and death. You must concentrate on being the only personality you can be and doing it well.

If the lesson of today is too much for one session, you can break it into several, but you must complete it before you enter into the meditation that precedes the next session.

Chapter Eleven

If you are to last your lifetime, this is the time to totally renew your body. Regardless of how old you are when you read this, we are asking you to refrain from doing anything detrimental to your health. We are not here to ask you to quit smoking or drinking alcohol, but if you do, you will be rewarded by gaining increased lifespan.

Why do you drink water? You are entirely made up of water and its components, but it is not necessary to drink water. We see you often forget to drink water, but do not know it is not the only thing causing you to thirst. Your life is not to be shortened by thirst, but thirst is not always due to a lack of water.

If you drink water, you can determine if the lack of water causes your discomfort. If you drink water and twenty minutes later you are still thirsty, you are hungry. Hunger is the reason you were thirsty. It is the imbalance of minerals and values of food that causes you to seek water. If water is not given, you fear starvation. If you are alert to the need for water and do not drink, you eat too much. Why eat when water would satisfy your need? If you drink water first to determine if you are hungry, your body will not gain excess weight.

If you ask: "If the body is obese and cannot reduce itself, how am I to enjoy life?" You do not care if your body is healthy. You care only about the shape of your body and if the other sex finds you attractive. This is vanity. Vanity is a means to get you to take care of you. Therefore, vanity is not necessary, but it helps some people eat correctly. Vanity is for fools, but it does help fools improve and seek to shed weight or gain strength. For this reason, we are not here to condemn vanity. We will not pass judgment on it.

Whatever you are or wish to be is seen first in the inner mind, but the inner mind cannot visualize what it has not seen. If you wish to gain insight into the real work of your body, study it. Dream on it. Visualize the corpuscles and veins pumping clean blood into the heart and circulating it into a body filled with air and water that is not polluted. Once you can visualize that, you can begin to cleanse the toxins from your system. Without ability to see, you are blind, but blindness is not the same as sightlessness. Some have no sight but see, while others see but are blind.

You are blind until you can see

When you decide to examine *you*—as you study our words now—you will determine whether or not you are healthy. If your answer is 'Yes' –very good. If the answer is 'No', we are here to help you start a new life today. It is that simple! You decide to renew your body, and we can help you.

THE WORK BEGINS

Good health relies on a strong, supple body with the ability to clear out waste frequently, and breathe deeply. If your bowels do not work well, you clog the entire system. For this reason, we start there.

Begin each morning the same and end each night improved. Once the body can change its routine, you will begin and end each day improved, but that takes a considerable amount of time in some cases.

Eat a little food to begin the day to get the internal glands moving and devouring the material that floats through the bowel. If you can eat less than the body requires for energy, you burn off weight faster. If you insist upon eating big meals, your body will continue to lose its ability to burn energy effectively. We urge you to begin each day with a little bit of cereal, since it is grain and has no fat. Once the day begins and food is digesting, the work of the brain begins in earnest. You are not lazy, but you cannot fully function on little food. It is so obvious, but how many today listen to their bodies?

If your body is hungry, you will learn little. You need energy to study and grow, yet many parents feed nothing to their children in the morning and prepare lunches meant to free them of annoying complaints from their offspring, instead of being in charge of serving nutritious food. You are spoiling a child if you do not take time to serve food on a regular basis. The child will grow into a demanding and irritated fool rather than a regular, well-balanced individual.

A sure sign a person has been spoiled in the past? If The World is not interested in you, you may decide The World is not very nice, or if The World delights in you, you may decide The World is not that great or it would be doing more for you. If you are spoiled, you need to regain your balance or achieve it.

To maintain a healthy body requires discipline and an earnest desire to be the best you can be. Even if you are not interested in your body, we are. We need a good mind to work with, and a good mind cannot live—let alone grow—in a sick body. To eat and eat and never develop is a sad commentary on modern living, but it is true that many are not growing in health due to poor nutrition.

How can you ignore your body?
It makes no sense to us!

The first step is to clean out your bowels. If you do not clean out the tubing regularly, it will become impacted with waste. It is disgusting to discover your body is full of waste, but it is if you do not cleanse the bowel regularly.

A method often used by man to clear the bowel is to irrigate it and let it expend the water and waste violently. This is not a good method. It is fast, but does harm. You must not let your bowel become so clogged that you need to soften the waste in order to painlessly eliminate it.

THE WORK BEGINS

The work of the mind is such that it can control the bowel and all its contractions. Why not use your head? You have a brain that can do this. Why use tools to do what your mind can easily control? The method we wish to see you use:

- Work out a plan to daily create a state of peace of mind.
- Once the mind relaxes, visualize the bowel as smooth and easy to clean—not clogged.
- By simply working on the bowel mentally, you can make it move continually and more easily work out anything in it.
- Relaxation is the key to bowel movement. Once the mind is relaxed, the body is also relaxed.
- The bowel is a long continuous muscle, and muscle is unable to relay impulses from the waste to the brain, but the brain can relay impulses to the waste and eliminate it.

The time to eliminate toxins is very close at hand now. All the food you eat circulates in your body and that food is full of poison. Poison is anything foreign to your mind or body. If you do not detoxify such material, it can harm or even kill the body. The body is not ready to die, so it carries on war every day with such material and causes you to feel *dis-ease*. This *dis-ease* is to let you know you must take immediate action.

Why are you reluctant to discover why you feel weary or unable to fully function? If you can remove toxins from your body on a regular basis, feeling great is your reward. A good way to filter out poison is to encapsulate it and vent it through the system. The capsulation of poison can be done by surrounding it with good food free of elements that would collect and distribute the toxic qualities of the poison. This can help:

- Eat grain that has no properties removed.
- Eat potatoes or fruits that have no allergens.
- Eat no meat while toxins are in the system, since meat requires a longer period to digest.
- Drink water to flush the system and eat less fat and sugar.

You will notice the difference immediately. Sugar is incapable of increasing your attention span or causing you to act *crazy*, but it can influence the digestion of toxins in your diet.

We will now end the debate on sugar! You are not to eat a lot of sugar, but it has no harmful properties. The harm done to your bodies by products that imitate sugar are far greater than any harm done by sugar. You need not eat sugar, but you crave these artificial sweeteners. End this dependency and enjoy better health.

What you need to do to increase your enthusiasm is add life to your body. Once the body is full of energy, the body sheds excess weight carefully and quickly. If the body is low on energy, it cannot get into high gear, as you say, and work hard. Be sure to eat the best food, if you want to treat your body as well as you treat your other means of locomotion.

When the body is full of gas, you fear death. That is why you must not let gas pockets accumulate in your body. The body can eliminate such pockets if air is discharged through the proper channels. Pockets develop when air cannot circulate through the stomach, bowels, and upper regions easily. You need to remove any obstruction to breathing or digesting food to avoid this problem.

To eliminate obstructions is not as easy as it sounds. First, you must not smoke while eating. It is the worst way to confuse the body. If you have to smoke, be sure you are not eating and digesting food. After that, the worst thing is to block air by sitting hunched over instead of standing and letting your body unkink its passages naturally. What is so difficult about either of these ideas that so many refuse to follow such simple instructions, and as a result, suffer from the effects of gas?

The circulation of blood is a problem when hastening to work and then suddenly slowing down. You need to decide what you want to do and do it. Do not start out at one pace, and then jump to another and another. It confuses the heart. After all, if you are to remain here on Earth enjoying a good life, you need your heart. If the heart is not maintained, you may think you can get a new one, but that is not wise to imagine. You should place your trust in God and ask for life instead of a new heart. If you request life, you will get it.

The worry of your mind is at such a high degree now that the entire planet is concerned over wars of spirit and body, yet wars of the planet are all caused by your minds. Why not change your minds? Is that such a difficult thing to do?

We think you make life difficult, because you are bored. Why let boredom into your life? Act and boredom cannot find a place to stay. You are in charge of your body's activity thus if you idle it is you who are bored—not your body. Idleness is not only bad for the mind, but the body believes it is not needed and begins to shut down. This premeditated slowdown can result in your body not responding when it is necessary to take action. If your body is tense, let it relax. If it is tired, rest. At all other times—keep it moving!

No words can make a heart beat, but thoughts can. If your thoughts are so easy to control, why neglect such an important pump? We see many control your anger and inflict pain upon yourselves. Why? Why fear anger? Anger is the sensation of pain you feel when your inner life is disturbed. It is not an evil emotion. It contains important messages the mind needs to evaluate in order to determine what you need to do to remove the pain. If you withhold such emotion, you cause pain to continue. The continuance of anger can cause the body to short circuit and delay emergency responses required to ease you out of danger.

Danger is not always from the outside world

Danger usually exists in the mind only, but that is where The World actually exists. If danger is in your mind, then you need to be on guard for all signs of disturbance, yet not relay false messages to the brain. Saying you are in no danger when you are is stupid, nor are you wise to let others continue hurting you.

Fight back if necessary to stop any attack on you. Never let another human stalk or attack you without resisting to your fullest ability. To let others grasp and shake you and declare you to be useless is to permit them to do harm to your soul. You must never let anyone harm your soul.

If a person kills another in anger, the attack is not premeditated, but must be punished. If the attack that kills another is premeditated, it should be punishable by the death of the attacker. To ignore such behavior is the downfall of your societies today. You need to decide if life is valuable or not; and if you decide to continue to ignore such violence, you will ALL have to answer for it—not just the perpetrators.

Many who did violence to the planet are still on Earth, and you care not if they are punished. The work of God cannot be destroyed by man. In order to end such destruction, you will all struggle to overcome the greed and dishonesty surrounding your lives or be taken to task for it at crossing over when you die.

Health of everyone is affected when fires rage and air becomes polluted—and when water is drained to feed only a few. This mismanagement of resources provided for all is not to be charged against everyone. The few responsible for it will be punished. That is a foregone conclusion that escapes many humans who revel in wasting water now. We will not belabor that point now, but it will be noted you have been warned.

Why would anyone want to be short? Why would anyone want to be obese? Why would anyone want to be bald? Are these insane questions? No, but you ask them all. If the point of living on Earth is to be a beauty queen, how could you achieve it if everyone was beautiful? You are not here to decide why you look like you do. You are here to rise above handicaps or distracting features that mar your physical beauty. If you cannot rise above it, you have to sit around for another life. We do not want that to happen again.

Wake up! See You! See life as it is and do not worry about others' lives. This is your life and others are in charge of their lives—not yours. You are not to be afraid of being different, but do not strive to be different. The maiming and mutilation of the body done in ancient times was to prove the body was not important, but maiming and mutilation done today is to say the body is what counts most. You must be stupid to think we care about your body when we do not even have bodies!

If your life is difficult, you need not say why it is difficult—that often makes it worse. If your life is easy, share the ways you learned to cope. Others need to be encouraged, not discouraged. You are not interested in others' problems and terrors, so why would they be interested in yours?

Now the time is approaching when the work of The World is over and all are to be graded. What do you think your best class will be? Will it be the one in which you star or the one in which you made the most progress so far? The only class to be examined is the one you fail.

We are not interested in turning you into the perfect human, but you should be. We do not care if you fall away from the crowd and enjoy life less, but you should care. Why are *you* on Earth?

We are here to help you expand and grow. Unfortunately, you are lost most of your lives. Act like adults quickly—rather than later in life. Assume you know what you are here to do and maybe you will turn out to be right. If you are not, nothing was wasted while you waited for your orders.

Not to be allowed to die would be a terrible thing, but to pursue suicide is worse. You are not here to deliver a life and then bow out of it. You are here to learn how to live. If you leave before you learn, you lose. You never learn if you never live, so give up killing or maiming yourself in order to avoid living now.

Disabilities are often seen as accidents, but seldom are. You know inside your mind you are not as bad off as you say, but by saying you cannot, you become disabled. It is a vicious cycle not worthy of man. Become angry at the work and leave, but do not shoot yourself in the foot to show you are angry. Work is not to be abandoned while you are on Earth. You will have to come back again to finish it, so get busy now and avoid such a delay in the development of your soul.

When free of disease, you can grow and develop emotionally and mentally. Disease cannot stop you from developing spiritually. Your mind is not the same as your Spirit, nor is the mental process the same as spiritual growth. Before you can increase your potential and possible growth, you must put aside such comparisons. The mind is here on Earth, but The Holy Spirit always exists.

Ruth Lee, *Scribe*

Whatever you do, do it for you!

We are here only to inspire you to work. You do the work necessary for the development of *you*, but we can help make life simpler. Act like a human and you will be human, but to act like a god does not come even close to becoming God. You are here to be human, so get it together now and let us all move on to the great work.

The work of the soul is not only here and now, but exists in all places and times. Actually, only Earth has time. You are not here, but you are. If you can grasp this, all the rest is easy.

We want you to develop your mind and body so Spirit can be free to do its work. If your mind or body is incapacitated, Spirit will make up the difference. Be kind to you, we love *you*.

Let us all depart into the center of our beings and meditate. If you do not feel peace, then let us all work on any area that still cannot function as intended. Begin by understanding the joy of being *you*—and life is then full of delight.

We will return once you complete your meditation. Then your mind is free of worry. Until you can go forward—meditate.

Chapter Twelve

The World is now ready for the beginning of the next world, but you are not—and you must not believe you are. You will be ready when the end is here. If the world is ready, how can you be otherwise?

We see your perception is that you create and it appears, but that is not true. You create perceptions, but not reality. You can alter the state of the universe, but not create the universe. You are unable to create anything!

The test:
What do you do that is yours alone?
Nothing!

You cannot create a thing. You must start with the germ of an idea. That germ is not from *you*—it is from God. You are only an instrument of God.

When the work of your hands is satisfying, you feel fine. If the work of your mind is satisfied, you feel like working—which is why you work. However, you will never be satisfied with your work and will never finish working. You are here to work. You are not here to sit and ask questions.

If questions you ask are not answered by us,
You are expected to work and find the answers

Wherever the work of God is—God is. If you are not of God, why would your work be of God? Simple answer: You are of God! You are here and will continue to exist.

God is not a simple idea. It is too complex for humans to comprehend, so it is suggested that you spend your time doing your work and ignore the work of God. If you do decide you must do God's work, you have to relive your life. This is why we want you to do your work now, so you can go forward to the next plane and do not have to relive this life.

The call to do God's work is not the call to do God's work. We refer to *the call* as doing God's work first, but still doing your work. If you do God's work, you neglect your own work. Besides, how do you know what God's work is?

If you do not answer our questions,
We are unable to answer yours!

Now that the air is clear around you, how do you clean air? We are unable to help you. We are forbidden to erase a thing. We were sent to be your instructors and teachers, but forbidden to step in and do your work.

You will be judged. You will be asked at the end to explain why you did not do much now. If your answer is unsatisfactory, the work is to be done over. You will be sent back. This is not The Way! The Way is to work now to clear the atmosphere and block further deterioration of Earth.

If you can stop only one thing, let it be the day of destruction. If Earth could be controlled and left alone, it would heal itself, but that takes centuries of your time. We cannot see that happening. You will never be able to see that time. It is not to be. You are to reign on Earth only as long as you take care of your subject—and that time has ended.

When Earth was created, God let you enjoy all of it. The Earth is a separate and individual planet. It is not the only planet, but it is the only one like it. You are different from every other human, too. If Earth is a separate and individual entity, why would you regard it as different from humanity?

The idea that you are the only living things on Earth is preposterous. You are living on a living thing! Earth lives! Earth is greater than all humanity combined, but Earth does not destroy itself. It grows and sheds its superfluous material, but it never destroys itself. You fear the shedding of lava and fear its rumbles, but Earth is not destroying itself.

You are destroying Earth!! If you stop, Earth could return to its original form, but we see you as unable to indulge our wishes. You prefer to indulge your appetites for pleasure and vice. You prefer to engage in practices that rape and pillage the land and people.

You are not entirely free of blame if you sit back and let people of your society destroy Earth and others. You are a member of that society. You are responsible for the behavior of your society. You are never to be overlooked or released because you were law-abiding and innocent. The parties of the second part are always as responsible as the parties of the first part. Is that not so?

We wonder why you constrict your movements. We also wonder why you are unable to bleach your soul of the stains of the past. If you cannot cleanse your soul, who will? The body is always your responsibility to cleanse, as well as the soul. You cleanse the soul in a totally different way than you clean your hair and body, but it is just as necessary.

We see people wash their hair daily. It is a ritual that produces loose skin that flakes off; nevertheless, they continuously clean. Why would a person clean their hair until it is damaged? It is an act of contrition. To clean the hair and body as a ritual is different from cleaning it to free oneself of pain or worry.

We suggest all who work in surroundings of pain and sorrow or evil should cleanse immediately upon leaving these people. Otherwise, daily cleansing is not so necessary since some cannot quickly restore the protective surfaces of their body and, as a result of destroying the surface of their skin, are subject to cancer.

When you are upset, you shower often and surgically alter your body. You also cut and groom your hair and face constantly. Does any of this change *you*? No. It helps the mind believe you are different—that you are better than before, but it does not change *you*. You need to be cleansed by The Holy Spirit for the soul to feel better.

Whatever you do, do it with vigor. Do not wash your body and let it go. Do not wash your hair and let it go. Do not wash out your mind and let it go. We are not here to clean up your act—you are.

You are expected to develop you *and* your soul. If you do not do it now, you must come back. If this is the only time you are on Earth, and it should take only one time, why are you not changing yourself? If you are unable to dwell on these things, we suggest you do not go any further right now. You are behind in your work. You will need to go back and adjust your life.

No one else is to adjust you or correct you. That is a misconception. When you are adjusted, you see things quite clearly. You know who you are and why you are here. It is so simple you wonder why the rest are lost. If you are lost, you wonder how to get free of the past. You wonder how to gain peace of mind. You fret over silly, stupid things that have no real bearing on *you*. You continually pick fault with anyone who crosses your path. All of this is because you are unhappy.

We are ready to go forward, if you are

We will take forward all who are ready and able to do The Work. If you are not ready, go back and reread The Work. When it makes sense, and you can grasp the reality of *you*, come back to this point. We will wait for you.

This is the point where you begin to grow. You are not yet near the starting gate, but can sense life is a race. You can now see time is of no use to anyone but you. However, it is your way of gauging whether or not you are on schedule.

Once the race is over, time slows. Whatever the race, you cannot win. You are there only to complete the courses you set out to do. You will never beat anyone else or be able to say you won, because winners are determined at the time you cross over to the other side.

Whatever course you choose, you are the only one taking it. You are not here to do someone else's work or the work of another life. You may have things leftover to do from a previous life, but you still have this life's work to do. Whenever you start working on this life's work, you know it. You will feel a surge of power enter into work you do. You will fear no one and be in your best shape mentally and emotionally. To do this is to advance your soul. It should help you get into the best possible shape mentally and physically, but it cannot if your heart and soul are not interested in advancing now.

If you are not interested in your life, it is no life for *you*. Whatever you do—do it well! We cannot repeat that too much. You are not here to do life over and over again. Do everything once and go forward. Do not repeat and repeat anything just because it feels good to know what you are doing. That is false and promises you a comeuppance at the end.

If your life is not full of adventure and stimulation, you will still be *you*. If your inner life is dull and listless, the adventure and stimulation of the world will never increase *you*. You must change you. You must not rely on stimulation or exercise or adventure to act upon you and change your life. It can, but it is only one way of successfully developing an aspect of the life you are living now.

Whatever the time of day or night, you may work. It is only suggested you work during the day on worldly matters, but it can be at other times, too. To always be too literal is confining to The Holy Spirit.

You must adjust to all change. If change is a problem, then seek it out. If the change of time is too difficult, you are dying. Once you no longer can change, you will not live long. It is the sign that time is up and you are ready to go on to the next assignment.

If the work of day extends into night, you must allow for it and take time off to compensate for the intrusion into your time. However, if you do not truly work, you cannot take time off to explore the work of self and others, you then are behind in your work of The World—and it would harm you.

To constantly travel is no way to gain control of your life, but travel is an outstanding way to learn tolerance of all other people. If you are unable to understand others, we want you to travel. If you cannot understand yourself, we want you to stay home.

The work of your life is best accomplished in a single room. It is not necessary to live in a mansion. To live, you need only one small space to be free of all others. If you live in a mansion overrun by employees, you have no place of your own. You are never alone. You would be better off to sell it and move into the city and live upstairs of a shop where no one knows you then live in a suburban dwelling where all constantly run in and out of your abode.

The work of The World is not necessary, but you have all decided it confirms your existence. We are not here to change that, but we suggest you now change your ideals. Why not let all people work at home? Why not let all people sit at computers and work by themselves? We are not averse to that, but how would you learn to tolerate all others? Why would you care if your body and mind deteriorated? When would you meet suitable mates? When would you relax? When would you seek others of like mind? What would you eat if you had all day to eat? What else?? It is your turn now to fill in the answers.

If the work of your day is not over at night, you suffer. You do not rest. You edge up your day's work and end up tired. If you are tired, your work on self is never begun. We sense a fatigue in your life now that is caused by the barrage of violence all around you. It is not actual work, but it causes fatigue that grates on you and causes you to wear out.

Why permit a segment of the population to run wild? We see you are constantly confronted with moral and legal dilemmas. Why? Why are you concerned about the moral and legal rights of others if those rights in turn intrude into your life and prohibit you from living as you are meant to live?

We now sense fear. The full work of evil in the world has you subdued—why?

The work of The World is not evil. It is good. If you do not work, you will slip into evil. Your mind is not *protractive*. It cannot extend and go on and on without input. Your soul can continue growing if the mind or the body is in a state of decay, but the mind needs to be fed. The body's urges will force the individual to feed it, but the mind cannot urge you to do your work—only your soul can do that.

The work of evil is not for the godly and soul developers among you. It is for those who are not ready to advance and are mistaken about the reason why they are here on Earth. It happens! It happens, but it need not. If you help evil ones understand success is denied to all who are evil, evil stops.

※

No one on Earth is here to suffer

All want success and the ability to be respected; however, if legal avenues are blocked, some seek other ways. When you unblock the avenues that deny others success, you will gain a greater ability to develop yourself. If you deny them, your work is not going to succeed. You are responsible for the lives of those who might not otherwise be able to advance. If this sounds contradictory to what the message has been, you are not listening to the soul. You are not here for only *you*, but *you* are responsible for you alone.

The last way to cleanse your soul is to open the airways and let the speech of all be heard. The air is now filled with only a few who think they are in control. If all can speak, all will be better off and able to develop. The will of some is such that it deters the advancement of many. The only time to be on the air is when you have something positive to say. If time on the air is filled with negativity, you all are harmed. It may not appear that way, but it is true.

The soul of *you* and all other humans is advancing, but not yet fully developed. To let negative thoughts form and advance further than positive forms is stupid. You are positive beings learning to deal with negativity. You do not know how to control it, so be careful. If negative vibrations are not attuned to the positive, the ear is hurt and the mind is deeply disturbed. Your music is not always what hurts your ears, sometimes it is the intent of the musician.

We are not here to judge you,
You must judge your work

If your work does not pass, you are not as deeply disturbed about it as we are. We send you messages and see you are not interested. Why? Do you think you are special? You are not! You are exactly the same to us as all other people.

Spiritual Guides are not all able to control and correct their people—but God is. You will know if your Guides are at work. You do not fear them, but you should. You are not here to be alone without help, but if that help is destructive to you and you do not care if you do the work, Guides would be placed in a powerless position and chastised.

Your Guides are responsible for your passage through this plane and will work diligently to access your mind in order to help you quickly clear it; but if you do not give them access or let them help in other ways, your life is not easy or very happy.

Happiness is being able to talk to your Guides!

We are unable to express the relief experienced by people who can pray and meditate, and thus gain access to their own wisdom. If you have never gained peace of mind, you will never know happiness is *not* being dead emotionally—but being alive.

Drugs are used exclusively to alter the moods of people and do nothing for the mind. If the body has a need for a drug or herb, it will cure the body. If the body has no need for it, the drug or herb will cause a rise in *dis-ease*.

If you want to alter your mood, you must alter your mind. It is not difficult. Laugh! If you laugh, you alter your mood. It is being unable to laugh and sing and dance that makes you feel bad. The work of your mood is to tell you that you are unhappy. If you are not in tune, you feel sad or blue, as you say. If you are downhearted, it is because you are not being true to *you*. All the rest of the garbage you preach is nonsense. Once you do your own work, you are free of sadness!

Women and men locked into jobs of self-denial are sad. Women locked into confining marriages are depressed and unable to express themselves well. Men who are not loved enough are unable to live as normal human beings and often become brutes. Why? Why would you continue to live in such circumstances? It is your life, and if you are unhappy, you must change it.

You are not here to impress us or your fellow humans. We do not care if you pass or fail, but your Spiritual Guides care. Your Guides are unable to access you if you never silence the ego. If the ego is loud and obnoxious, you are not free of worry nor are you happy.

The ego is needed to navigate through this material world, but it is not in charge. The body is unable to develop if the ego does not take care to eat, exercise, and protect it—otherwise the ego does not run the body. The ego is not necessary for the mind to develop. The mind is not upset if the ego is chastised—believe it or not! The mind is upset if it is unable to think.

If the ego is in charge all day, let it rest at night. Let the ego slip into a sleep or trance or whatever you call your waking state where you do not listen to that noise in your head. We are unable to substitute anything into your way of thinking. We are unable to enter your thoughts, but you can think. So listen to us. Listen to your Guides. Listen to the wisdom of others who will help you, but do not listen intently to the nonsense the ego imposes upon you—instead restrict it to its own work.

If the ego is stronger than the mind, and it is certainly strong today in most people's lives, you will discover you are never satisfied. You want whatever you see. You want others to admire or concentrate on you only. You want power and fortune in order to control others. You are in a deadly state of war with yourself. You will be unable to learn the lessons necessary to advance, and you will fail life.

If the mind is stronger than the ego, which is seldom the case in most of your world, the body is taken care of and developed in order to obey the commands of the mind. The body is shared and used by all who know it can be of use in developing society. It is not reserved for the pleasure of another or used to hold back others. It is not as developed physically as the ego-driven person's body, but it is not out of shape either. The mind is the controlling element. Why you argue over that insignificant small idea is not important, but the argument itself is.

When you are ready to develop the mind and body simultaneously, we are ready to teach you how to advance. If the body is developed, then let us develop the mind. If the body is not developed, we cannot help. You are the only ones able to manipulate the material world. All of us are in spirit and unable to control or alter life. It is your responsibility to control you and your body.

If the body is not in shape or healthy, take it out of the closet and onto the road. Walking the body is soothing to it and does many other things for the mind. The driving of the body to destinations is not wise. The body arrives before the mind is ready. If you walk, the mind and body arrive at the same time. We prefer walking to running because it is not so strenuous, but if you walk so fast that it singles out certain muscles, we suggest you lope along. It is far less stressful.

If the body is in shape now, and you are free of stress and the mind is flowing, we are finally ready to begin work. The work of the soul is not hard, but it does require discipline. That is the lesson. Once your mind, body, and soul are disciplined, you are enlightened!

You will continue to finish living this life, but you will be advanced to the next plane. Once this life's work is done and you are assured of enlightenment, you must help others advance. That will advance *you* in the next plane.

Whatever you do, you are the only one who knows why you do it. If you want to reach enlightenment, you need only decide to do it. No one else can do it for you or prevent you from attaining it. It is totally your decision.

We do not wish to continue any further with this book, because you need to work on *you*. If we continue to write, you will continue to read and not do your work. If the work of the soul is to be done, the work of your life must be finished and development of your mind completed before it can begin. We will give you no problem you cannot find the answer to in your work on self, but you will be unable to find the answer if you only read about it.

From this time forth, you are in charge of the progress you make. We are conferring upon you the degree in advance. If you do not make it, your credentials will be stripped from you at the end—but we think not. We feel you will not to be stripped of anything you work hard to achieve.

Begin now to circulate into The World and see why you are unable to feel exactly like *you*. Once you learn that, you are there. The World is not necessary, but you are.

If *you* are to be free of guilt, prepare to clear the atmosphere and water of Earth, and then do it. The Earth is your project as a people, but your life is your total responsibility. We go in fear of nothing, but you have everything to fear if you do not work on *you*—so get to work!

Have You Read?

We Are Here
The Teachers of the Higher Planes
Ruth Lee, *Scribe*

First in *The Books of Wisdom* series scribed by Ruth Lee, **We Are Here** is the work of teachers from other spheres charged with educating humanity about the basic facts of life, spirituality, and ascension. *The Teachers* present material essential to living a full and meaningful life.

For those seeking answers to the fundamental questions of life, **We Are Here** provides all you need to ace this life and ascend to the next. *The Teachers* provide clear instructions on how to correct problems of Today, while pointing out areas that we alone can redo or work on together while here.

This work is revolutionary in its straight-forward presentation of what the world needs and how each person can achieve higher levels of love, success, and peace in all aspects of daily living.

We Are Here
A Must Read!

For more information, visit:
www.LeeWayPublishing.com

www.ingramcontent.com/pod-product-compliance
Lightning Source LLC
LaVergne TN
LVHW051637080426
835511LV00016B/2364